Railway Memories No

SHEFFIELD

STEPHEN CHAPMAN

....And Sheffield, smoke-involv'd; dim where she stands
Circled by lofty mountains, which condense
Her dark and spiral wreaths to drizzling rains.
Anna Seward 1747 - 1809

BELLCODE BOOKS
CHURCH VIEW, MIDDLE STREET.
RUDSTON, EAST YORKSHIRE YO25 4UF
email: bellcode4books@yahoo.co.uk

Edited by Steve Chapman

Printed in the UK by the Amadeus Press, Cleckheaton, West Yorkshire. BD19 4TQ

Proudly displaying the Master Cutler headboard, Leicester V2 2-6-2 No. 60863 starts from Victoria station and begins her journey to London Marylebone in the mid-1950s. *Tom Greaves*

FRONT COVER: One of Sheffield's most memorable expresses was the Harwich boat train and in steam days it could be relied upon to produce interesting motive power. For a long time it was entrusted to the B17 4-6-0s east of Sheffield and here B17/6 No. 61620 *Clumber* prepares to leave Victoria station in September 1958, after taking over from the electric loco which brought the train from Manchester. *Geoff Warnes/Colour-Rail*

BACK COVER TOP: The south end of Sheffield Midland in about 1971, before resignalling. Sheffield South No.2 signal box is on the right and Sheffield South No.1 on the left while the Class 08 shunts coal wagons. *Colour-Rail*

BACK COVER BOTTOM: The scene at Rotherwood Sidings on 7th July 1979 with Class 76 electrics present. *Stephen Chapman*

FRONTISPIECE: In the immediate pre-nationalisation era, begrimed LMS Jubilee No. 5679 *Armada*, of Millhouses shed, attracts little attention from the spotters as she prepares to take a southbound stopping service out of platform 7. *Tom Greaves*

Requests for photographs *published in Railway Memories will be passed automatically to the copyright holder and under normal circumstances Bellcode Books itself will not reply to readers making such requests.*

INTRODUCTION

One of Britain's biggest cities, centre of steel manufacturing, railway crossroads, and surrounded by steep hills on three sides, Sheffield needs no introduction.

Nowadays, its Midland station is an important and bustling interchange between long-distance and commuter services from far and wide, and Sheffield's railways are set to continue at the leading edge of railway technological progress.

But passengers are just about all its railways carry nowadays, along plain tracks uninterrupted by points, sidings, depots and freight yards since the devastating recession of the early 1980s, and the industrial collapse and railway retrenchment of the ensuing years.

This, the 27th in the Railway Memories series, takes us back to the times when Sheffield's two distinct railway systems ran steam expresses to all parts of the country, when boat trains ran to Harwich and Liverpool, electric trains to Manchester, and Pullman trains to King's Cross. Times when an intense industrial landscape spawned a daily cascade of up to 800 freight train movements rumbling and grinding their way around the city environs.

Most scenes are from the 1950s and 60s but in the usual Railway Memories style, they range from the 1930s to the early 2000s for even in the last 15 years or so, much more has become just a memory.

The pictures in this book come from a variety of originals, ranging from tiny contact prints, and old, deteriorated film

to black and white reproductions of colour slides, which renders some of them photographically imperfect, but the images they convey are rare and utterly priceless.

A peculiarity of this area, and perhaps others, is that railway spellings of place names often differ from the local version, the suffix "brough" and "borough" often being a subject of debate. Wherever this occurs, the spelling used in railway documents is normally the one used in Railway Memories.

On 7th September 1964, British Railways began using the 24-hour clock in its working timetables so we use am/pm up to that date and 24-hour times thereafter.

The Great Central "Director" 4-4-0s were a familiar part of the Sheffield railway scene with the last English "Large Director" D11s ending their days at Darnall in 1960. Yet to receive British Railways livery, D10 No. 2657 *Sir Berkeley Sheffield*, a Trafford Park engine, receives attention at Darnall shed on Easter Sunday 11th April 1948. The workmanship of the "not to be moved" disc alone is worthy of note. *Neville Stead collection*

3

Steel roads from the steel city

Given its topographical situation, Sheffield's growth into one of Britain's largest cities, world renowned centre for production of high quality steels, busy railway hub and its ability to carve a place in the post-industrial age, has been nothing short of miraculous and stands as a tribute to the determination and prowess of its sons and daughters from the Victorians to the present day.

Growing up around the confluence of several fast-flowing small rivers, the best known of which are the Sheaf and the Don, and with ironstone in the surrounding tree-covered hills, Sheffield was perfectly situated on a supply of water power and raw materials for iron making. By the 14th century it was noted for its knives and by 1600 had become England's principal centre for cutlery manufacture, providing a springboard for the great steel industry for which it is renowned. But it took 19th century Yorkshire grit and determination in good measure to overcome the natural obstacles which threatened to hold back Sheffield's industrial progress. Blocked from the west and south by uplands rising to 1700ft it was effectively cut off from fast growing markets in London, the Midlands and Lancashire. The only level route out of Sheffield was northwards, via the Don Valley.

The coming of the steam age, the presence of coal, nearby limestone and great leaps in methods of mass producing steel - not least local steelmaker Henry Bessemer's converter - fuelled an explosion of industry throughout the area. But without better transport links Sheffield risked being left behind. Knives and cutlery may be easily taken to markets by packhorse - the only realistic form of transport over the hills to the south and west - but pack horses were no use for the much bigger wealth-creating manufactured goods that Sheffield needed to be producing if it was to really prosper. By 1819 Sheffield had a canal to the heart of the town but by then the railway age had already begun. Just 35 miles away, steam locomotives had started hauling coal on the Middleton Railway in Leeds seven years before.

Sheffield's earliest recorded rail transport was a two-mile wooden waggonway from the Duke of Norfolk's coal pits on Park Hill, dating from at least 1729, to a coal yard in the town. In the 1770s it was replaced by what is believed to be the first cast iron plateway, invented by the colliery's engineer John Curr, running down from the Duke's newly-sunk Manor Colliery and alongside Blast Lane to Manor coal yard. It was still shown on the 1855 Ordnance Survey map. Other early tramroads ran to the canal from coal pits in Tinsley Park and Handsworth.

By the 1830s Sheffield's population had grown to over 91,000 but it looked like being sidelined when the first main line railway to the area was proposed. The North Midland Railway from Derby to Leeds would serve Rotherham - but not Sheffield. Its engineer George Stephenson was charged with building a fast, level main line and to serve Sheffield would demand gradients too steep for locomotives over the hills to the south, therefore requiring slow, tedious inclines which he was determined to avoid. To the consternation of Sheffield's civic and business leaders it went via the Rother Valley, east of Sheffield, through Eckington, Killamarsh and Treeton to Rotherham. Thus began a dissatis-faction with the city's London rail links that would last 150 years. Stephenson told Sheffield's leaders that if they wanted a railway they should build their own branch to the NMR. This did not go down well and some proposed their own lines to the south, but the 5.25-mile Sheffield & Rotherham Railway went ahead.

Completed on 1st November 1838 - the first railway in both towns - it ran from its Sheffield terminus at Wicker to its own Rotherham terminus in Westgate. Pre-dating the North Midland by 18 months, it began as an isolated line but a connection with the Earl Fitzwilliam's Greasbrough Colliery waggonway at Parkgate, north of Rotherham, enabled the movement of coal by rail right into Sheffield, thus breaking a monopoly held by the Duke of Norfolk.

The North Midland opened between Derby and Masborough on 11th April 1840 and between Masborough and Leeds on 1st July. From its station at Masborough, Rotherham now enjoyed direct trains to Leeds, York, the Midlands and London while Sheffield remained at the end of a branch line. It wasn't totally left out though. With a connection to the North Midland at Masborough, the NMR began operating from Wicker alongside the S&R's Sheffield-Rotherham service. It was now possible to travel by train from Sheffield to London via Derby in nine and a half hours. It wasn't perfect, often involving an excessive wait at Masborough, but it put Sheffield on the emerging national rail network, opening up access to materials and markets across the country.

Within five years of the S&R's opening - by which time both railways had merged with others to form the Midland Railway - five major iron and steel firms had established themselves between Sheffield and Rotherham as the rural districts of Grimesthorpe, Brightside and Meadow Hall began their transformation into dense complexes of industry. It has been said that by 1851, 86 per cent of Britain's cast steel was being produced in Sheffield and the railways were now contributing to the town's growth in more ways than one. The demand for steel rails during this rapid railway expansion era drove the innovation of more efficient mass production methods. In fact, it was John Brown's Atlas Works at Brightside that pioneered the mass production of steel rails.

But Sheffield urgently needed improved transport to Liverpool if it was to maintain its dominant position as an exporter of bladed tools and cutlery. Various eccentric and unworkable schemes were proposed until, spurred by huge potential demand in Lancashire for Yorkshire coal, the Sheffield, Ashton-under-Lyne and Manchester Railway was incorporated in 1837. Although challenging, its proposed route was realistic and would go ahead to become Sheffield's first true main line. It followed the route from a terminus at Bridgehouses to Manchester via Penistone and Woodhead. It could not avoid steep gradients and sharp curves on the climb from Sheffield but it did avoid inclines. The physical obstacles to be overcome, not least the 3mile 22yd Woodhead Tunnel, were huge, many, and costly in both money and more than 50 lives, not least because of cholera spread by squalid conditions in the navvies' camps. An economic recession compounded an ongoing shortage of funds and the project was nearly leased to the Midland Railway which would have had interesting implications for Sheffield's railways in the future. The line opened throughout in December 1845 upon completion of the Woodhead Tunnel, Britain's longest at the time and consisting of one bore conveying a single track under the Pennines, a second bore being added in 1852. Sheffield was now connected directly to the North West. In 1847 the Midland opened a short, steeply graded branch connecting the SA&MR at Bridgehouses to its Wicker terminus. The line was so steep it would only be used for transferring goods wagons.

Within a year of the Woodhead line's opening, the Sheffield & Lincolnshire Junction Railway was authorized, the first stage

On the route of the Sheffield & Rotherham Railway, York V2 2-6-2 No. 60961 lollops through Brightside station with the 8.40am Bristol-Newcastle at 1.1pm on Saturday 23rd June 1962. *Robert Anderson*

between Bridgehouses, Woodhouse and a junction with the Midland at Beighton opening in February 1849. Its engineering features included a 660ft-long stone viaduct in Sheffield over roads, the Don and the canal which included the 72ft-span Wicker Arch over Wicker Road. Another was the 36-arch Rother Viaduct, completed only after heavy rain had combined with sub-standard construction to cause the collapse of 21 arches. Five months later, the line was completed through to Worksop, Retford and Gainsborough where it met the Great Grimsby & Sheffield Junction Railway, forming a direct route from Manchester to Grimsby. During the course of construction, these two companies had merged with the SA&M on January 1st 1847 to form the Manchester, Sheffield & Lincolnshire Railway.

Having been granted running powers to Bridgehouses by the MS&L, the Great Northern Railway ran a Lincoln service from 1850 that connected with King's Cross trains and until 1858 the Midland made use of the Beighton connection with through carriages between Bridgehouses and Euston Square. In 1851, Bridgehouses was replaced by the new Victoria station. The following year the GN completed the final section of its East Coast main line and a connection to the MS&L at Retford opened up a much shorter route between Sheffield and Kings Cross.

Over the next 20 years new routes were opened from Sheffield to Barnsley, Mexborough and Doncaster, plus a number of local branches. Finally, in February 1870, the city got its direct route to

the Midlands and London when the Midland Railway completed its new main line from a junction with the Sheffield & Rotherham at Grimesthorpe to the North Midland line at Tapton Junction, Chesterfield. It required the 1 mile 264yd Bradway Tunnel through the hills south of Dore, a 1 in 100 ruling gradient out of Sheffield for five miles, and a grand new station in Pond Street. Ponds had to be drained before the station could be built and even then it had to stand over the confluence of the rivers Sheaf and Porter, with a consequential risk of flooding which it has suffered in recent times. Many major works were needed with immense local disturbance. South of the city, a thousand newly-built working class homes had to be demolished. North of the new station, a long, deep cutting had to be hewn through rock and 15 overbridges constructed because old mine workings and sandstone quarries made tunnelling impossible. To the south again, the Duke of Norfolk forced the Midland Railway to cover the line and build an ornamental terrace where it crossed his property. Costs soared to almost three times the original estimate but at least it was good practice for the Midland's ultimate challenge which was about to follow, and which when completed would put Sheffield on an Anglo-Scottish main line - the Settle & Carlisle. When the new line opened, like Bridgehouses, Wicker station was closed to passengers and rebuilt as a goods depot while the original NMR route became known to generations of railwaymen as "The Old Road."

Sheffield was now riding high. The steel industry was booming,

The impressive and stylish Wicker Arch, a railway structure forming an iconic gateway to the city. Within the buildings on the right was an entrance to Victoria station while immediately beyond the arch is the site of the Sheffield & Rotherham's Wicker station. The Royal arms are in stone on the left and the Master Cutler's on the right. The MSLR's crest is on the far side. *Stephen Chapman*

it had two principal main lines and two main line stations, and in 1893 with the population nearing 450,000, having more than trebled since the opening of its first railway, it was granted city status. But two further developments were to come which would complete the transformation of this isolated town into a major industrial centre at the heart of England's rail network. That same year, the Midland completed the Dore & Chinley Railway after taking it over when it failed to attract the necessary capital. It required construction of the 3 mile 950yd Totley Tunnel - Britain's second longest after the Severn Tunnel - and the 2 mile 182yd Cowburn Tunnel - 9th longest. At Chinley it joined the Midland's Derby-Manchester main line, providing a second route to Manchester and passenger services began in June 1894.

Finally, in 1899 the MS&L completed its direct main line to London Marylebone, virtually shadowing the Midland's St. Pancras route. At the same time the MS&L changed its name to The Great Central Railway which, along with the Midland would dominate Sheffield's railways in an atmosphere of bitter rivalry and splendid isolation from each other.

Having outlined the early beginnings of Sheffield's railways, we can now explore them by joining an imaginary inspection special around the network as it might have been in 1955.

Our saloon is M45045, one of the standard London Midland & Scottish Railway saloons, and our engine is 2P 4-4-0 No. 40538 specially turned out by Millhouses shed. With 40538 propelling, we have a clear view of the road ahead as we leave Rotherham Masborough along Sheffield's first railway. Entry to the Sheffield area is marked ignominiously by the Sheffield Corporation sewerage works at Blackburn Meadows, just below on our left. Its extensive standard gauge internal railway has connections to the neighbouring GC line for sludge trains that run to a tip near Thrybergh, north of Rotherham.

Wincobank Up sidings on our immediate left are followed by Wincobank North Junction and, on our right, the Down sidings comprising something like 26 dead-end roads. From the junction a line runs parallel on our right and after we cross over the GC route to Barnsley it curves away over a viaduct forming a connection to the Midland's Barnsley line. Beyond it are Wincobank gas works and the works of the Yorkshire Engine

Company, builders of steam and diesel locomotives, mainly for industry and export.

After passing Wincobank station, due to close next year, we are joined by two branches coming in towards Sheffield from the right. The first, at Blackburn Valley Junction is the original Barnsley line, opened by the South Yorkshire Railway in September 1854, the short section from Meadow Hall Junction now only used by local trip freights. Next is Wincobank Station Junction where the Midland line from Barnsley joins us, now the only one carrying passenger trains. This line began life in 1893 as a goods branch to Thorncliffe Iron Works, Chapeltown, but was extended to Barnsley and opened to passengers in July 1897.

Behind a bank on our left now is a mass of foundries, heavy engineering works and steel plants such as Hadfields' East Hecla Works, Edgar Allen's Imperial Steel Works, William Cooke's and Cooper & Turner's rivet and brass works. They are squashed into an area of about half a square mile between the Midland and GC lines. Within that space a tangle of industrial railways wanders around the great buildings but they are not connected to our line.

Shortly, we pass through inappropriately-named Brightside station and junction where we are joined from the left by the Sheffield District Railway to which the dense mass of works is connected. Now we enter a congested corridor of steel and heavy engineering plants. First, on our left, the English Steel Corporation's River Don Works. On our right is Upwell Street goods yard, followed by the ESC's Grimesthorpe Works, with sidings alongside us from which lines disappear into the works buildings. This massive works is still with us as we pass the extensive Brightside Sidings on our left with Grimesthorpe carriage and wagon shops behind them. Sheffield motive power depot is next. At Grimesthorpe Junction we take the Wicker goods branch while the 1870 Chesterfield line curves away gently to the left. Cardigan sidings are on our left now; on the right are Engine Shed Sidings - so named because the original Grimesthorpe engine shed was here. Now, we plunge into a dark and smoky avenue of towering steel plants. Thomas Firth & John Brown's huge Atlas Works and Blast Furnaces dominate both sides, followed by Kayser, Ellison & Co's Carlisle Works on our right. Spear & Jackson's Etna Works is also here. We are reminded of Daniel

Defoe's portrayal of 18th century Sheffield in his travelog *A tour through the whole island of Great Britain*: "The town of Sheffield is very populous and large, the streets narrow, and the houses dark and black, occasioned by the continued smoke of the forges, which are always at work."

After passing under Sutherland Street, the second of two overbridges, the ESC's Cyclops Works is on our right as the scene ahead opens out into Wicker goods yard. There are around 30 sidings, one with a travelling overhead crane, four pairs of sidings with cartage roads between each pair, and eleven going into a large goods shed standing straight ahead of us. The yard is packed with goods vans, open wagons and containers on flat wagons. On the right of the goods shed one line continues into Spital Hill Tunnel, being the disused goods spur up to the GC at Bridgehouses. With a gradient of 1 in 36, only a handful of wagons could be moved at a time. Built by the "cut and cover" method, the 300yd tunnel achieved infamy in 1861when the roof caved in, killing six workmen. Our Victorian plan shows two tracks entering it whereas we see only a single line tunnel. Over the years, it had to be relined and strengthened to the point where it was reduced to single track.

Having covered the Sheffield & Rotherham, our 2P hauls us back to Grimesthorpe Junction where we continue along the main line, propelled again, towards Sheffield along embankments and through Attercliffe Road station, its platforms up above the streets.

We pass under Victoria station's eastern approach lines and then plunge into the narrow rock trench that is Nunnery Cutting. Over our heads is a succession of bridges. Most carry roads but two more are railways. The first overbridge after the lines into Victoria carries the National Coal Board's Nunnery Colliery Railway to a coal yard on the site of Sheffield Colliery, next to Blast Lane. We

then come to Nunnery Main Line Junction signal box, trapped in the shadows and engulfed in smoke - pity the poor signalmen who spend their shifts here. At least there is light from a gap in the rock face on our left where the sharp curve from Nunnery carriage sidings comes down at 1 in 60. The Midland Railway opened this branch in 1870 and it formed a direct connection for goods traffic with the MS&L up above. In 1886 it extended to Nunnery Colliery. Clearly the Midland did not take kindly to the MS&L establishing its own main line to London in direct competition because by 1898 it had severed the connection and since then the MS&L line can only be reached by shunting through the sidings.

At this point we pass under another bridge carrying a branch opened in February 1903 by the London & North Western Railway to its City goods station. Directly above it is another road bridge carrying Navigation Hill. A signal brings us to a stand and after what seems like an eternity, a Jubilee 4-6-0 blasts purposefully past us with an express, the crimson and cream livery of its carriages just managing to penetrate the floating smog.

The signal eventually clears and we continue beneath bridge after bridge. The gloom gives way to daylight as the tracks fan out before us into the nine platforms of Sheffield Midland station, the arched trainshed roof over the original east side of the station towering above us. The roof is soon to be replaced by plain platform canopies such as those on the later west side. It is blackened and decrepit now with many missing pains of glass but must have been impressive when new. It was then widely known as Pond Street but officially was just plain Sheffield.

We are kept moving through the bustling station - the signalmen want us out of the way. On the right, at the south end of the platforms, a line trails back behind the station buildings into Pond

In the mid-1950s, Grimesthorpe-based 4F 0-6-0 No. 44212 lifts a trip freight past Nunnery Main Line Junction signal box and through the deep cutting which the Midland Railway had to dig in order to make a northern exit from its Sheffield station. *Tom Greaves*

Street goods yard, while in the south west corner are a loading dock, sidings and a turntable with roads radiating from it.

After a short tunnel(or long bridge) under Shrewsbury Road, we are in another cutting as we start our way along the Up Fast line. Above us, virtually out of view on the left is the Duke of Norfolk's former Sheffield residence, a castellated stately home known as "The Farm" and now railway offices of somewhat uncharacteristic appearance. The Midland had to buy it from the Duke in order to quadruple the line in the late 19th century. Below us on the right is the underpass carrying the Down Fast underneath the Local (Chinley)lines so that northbound trains can enter the west side of the station without being impeded by other traffic, and depart without having to cross the north end approaches. Queens Road goods yard spreads out beyond the Local lines.

On the 1 in 100 climb from Sheffield there are still works and factories, but mostly we see endless rows of houses and as we progress southward the view is increasingly one of leafy suburbs.

Having left Midland station about a mile and a half behind, we pass Heeley, the first of four suburban stations along this stretch. Not long after, on our left come the goods depot and carriage sidings. Next, on our right, comes Millhouses motive power depot, the Midland passenger shed and home to our loco. It nestles by the sylvan greenery of the Abbeydale district, a complete contrast to its goods engine counterpart at appropriately named Grimesthorpe. We pass Millhouses & Ecclesall station and under a road bridge, and that is the last we see of industrial Sheffield on this line. Woods and parks now border the line. We pass Beauchief station and then Dore & Totley where the Local lines diverge away towards Dore & Totley West Junction, Totley Tunnel and Chinley. The hills close in as we take a left curve to pass Dore South Junction where the line from Dore West, which enables trains to run direct between Chinley and Chesterfield, comes in from the right before we enter Bradway Tunnel.

Having reversed at Chesterfield, 40538 hauls us down the original North Midland line - the Old Road - to Killamarsh West. Shortly after the closed station are a jumble of connecting lines and junctions. First is Killamarsh Branch Junction where a line goes east to Norwood and Kiveton Park collieries. On our left are the remains of the mile-long Great Central branch to the now closed Holbrook Colliery. Then we pass under the Great Central main line from London. Up to our right a branch curves away from it and heads north east to Waleswood Junction on the Retford line. There are more junctions and lines here which we will visit later.

Turning left at Beighton Junction we join the GC main line. We see sidings on both sides before heading through closed Beighton station, followed by the Crown steel works on the right and then Beighton permanent way depot before joining the Retford line at Woodhouse Junction. Curving in sharply from the left into Woodhouse Sidings is the closed two and half mile branch from Birley Colliery, opened by the MS&L a century ago.

After Woodhouse station it is a very different railway for we are now under the wires of the newly electrified line to Manchester. We haven't gone far when a turntable on the right heralds the start of Rotherwood Sidings on both sides of the line. These have been installed for the purpose of exchanging freight train locomotives between electric to the west and steam to the east and south. The next railway landmark is a branch trailing away right, down a steep incline, to the Orgreave Colliery and Coke works. We now have sidings on our right until reaching the coking works and coal washery of Handsworth Colliery, about half a mile away to the south and connected by an internal mineral line passing over us.

Having travelled for a while through semi-rural surroundings, we re-enter the urban and industrial confines of Sheffield, marked by Darnall goods yard on the right and Darnall Engineering Works on our left. Prince of Wales Road passes underneath and then we negotiate the island platform of Darnall station. Cravens carriage

Climbing out of the underpass, Jubilee 4-6-0 No. 45612 *Jamaica*, of Kentish Town shed, emerges from beneath Shrewsbury Road bridge and into Midland station with a 1950s express from St. Pancras. *Tom Greaves*

Darnall motive power depot c1960 with Britannia Pacific No. 70003 *John Bunyan*, doubtless having arrived with the boat train from Harwich, sharing the yard with customary B1 4-6-0s, J11 0-6-0s and wagons of loco coal. How appropriate that Kettle Bridge was the vantage point for so much steam. *D. P. Leckonby*

and wagon works is on the right now and on the left begins the smoking expanse of Darnall motive power depot. This is the biggest and most modern in Sheffield, only 12 years old and including a maintenance shed for electric locomotives. At Darnall Junction a curve to Attercliffe Junction, on the Mexborough line, leaves us. After passing under Kettle Bridge, we are crossed by a single line flyover into Darnall depot which enables locomotives coming from Victoria station to access the shed clear of main line traffic. A single line on our left is for engines coming off shed.

At Woodburn Junction the line from Mexborough joins us on the right. From here to Victoria station is an almost incomprehensible expanse of sidings with Nunnery Colliery and coke ovens up on the left. A line goes left underneath the Nunnery Colliery lines and into Nunnery goods depot, opened by the LNWR in 1895 and originally named City Goods. From the approach to the company's yard runs the double track branch to its much bigger Wharf Street, passing through a tunnel en-route. When this goods station opened in 1903 it took the City name. Apparently, a building in Bernard Street used to be a hospital for the LNWR's cartage horses.

From the LNW yard, on the very southern edge of the expanse, a spur climbs up to the Sheffield Corporation abattoir alongside Nunnery Colliery Railway sidings. Two colliery lines leave the these sidings, one to the Blast Lane coal yard which passes over the Wharf Street branch before entering a tunnel, while the other comes in our direction to sweep secretively down an incline into a tunnel beneath the whole railway complex, underneath Lumley Street, over the canal and the River Don, and into a coke yard surrounded by foundries. Facing west with its back to the incline, is the LNWR's engine shed, a brick structure with a westlight roof and which once had four roads, but is now derelict after being disused since 1928.

The LNWR presence here is considerable to say it had no lines of its own into Sheffield, or anywhere nearby. It planned to build a line from its Stockport-Buxton branch to a station of its own in Sheffield but the MS&L, concerned at the commercial threat posed by

such a powerful competitor, gave the LNW running powers over its lines in return for the abandonment of its plan.

Nearest on our left are the Midland carriage sidings from which descends the curve to Nunnery Main Line Junction. From the east end goes the Midland line to Nunnery Colliery and parallel to it the GC colliery line. Meanwhile, on our right, are the extensive GC Bernard Road goods and carriage sidings.

We are now on one of about a dozen lines crossing over the Midland main line. On our left, lines feed into Park and Blast Lane goods depots while on the right is a turntable as we pass over the Sheffield & Tinsley Canal to arrive in Victoria station. With only five platforms it is half the size of Midland while its low, functional, trainshed roof was replaced by canopies during the electrification work. What it lacks in presence is made up by the adjacent Royal Victoria Hotel, built in red brick with profuse stone dressings. Even then, it appears more brash than stylish. The station's most outstanding feature as anyone having to run for a train knows, is the steep 320yd approach road.

We pause at Victoria long enough to take water; being an alien here, 40538 diverts attention from the gleaming new Co-Co electric arriving from Manchester. Restarting, we immediately cross the Wicker Arch and begin the 18.75-mile ascent up a ruling 1 in 120-135 gradient all the way to the Woodhead Tunnel. On our right a siding goes into one of two corn mills hereabouts, a reminder that it is not just Sheffield's furnaces that need feeding. It is followed on the left by sprawling Bridgehouses goods yard with its various goods sheds. The longest casts a shadow over us as we run alongside. On the other side, we see the disused branch down to Wicker, a cattle dock situated in the fork of its junction. Next come Harvest Lane coal drops on our left and then on the right, Neepsend carriage and wagon shops - the GC engine shed until replaced by Darnall. Behind it stand the Sheffield Brick Company's works where a narrow gauge incline leads from a clay pit. More sidings are on our right and Neepsend gas works on the left, followed by the site of Neepsend station, closed in 1940. Next

Immingham's K2 2-6-0 No. 61724 makes a rousing start up the climb from Sheffield as she storms past Bridgehouses with an Annesley-Mottram class J goods on Wednesday 3rd January 1951. *Alan Ashley*

on the left is the remnant of a line into Neepsend goods yard on Hoyland Road, the three-road warehouse and overhead travelling crane obliterated during an air raid in 1940 which devastated the area when German bombs ignited an estimated three million cubic feet of gas stored at the gas works. On the right we can see Parkwood mine which extracts ganister for use in fire bricks. Down below, the River Don tumbles down to the city as we cling part way up the north side of its valley. Its confluence with the River Loxley is down there and in the headland between the two are the Upper and Nether Slack steel and wire mills complete with internal railway but isolated from the main line.

As we wind past Neepsend power station a Sentinel steam loco is just visible between the rows of wagons. Town and industry give way to sports grounds and allotments but we are not out of city environs yet. Such appearances are deceptive as Sheffield retains much of the woodland it has grown up in since the earliest times. Needless to say it isn't long after crossing Herries Road by means of a stone viaduct noted for its five tall arches that we re-enter built-up surroundings with sidings on our right, and beyond them a large claypit with narrow gauge incline leading into a brickworks as we approach Wadsley Bridge. The station is open but sees most of its passengers when Sheffield Wednesday are playing at home, or when a neutral venue is needed for a cup tie, for the Hillsborough football ground is nearby. Having passed the station with iron and steel works on each side and more sidings on the left, tennis courts, bowling greens and cricket fields - and the Hope and Anchor Brewery - appear below. Before long we pass between the British Acheson Electrode Works on our left and the Batchelor's pea canning factory on the right.

Now the landscape changes suddenly and dramatically, and we become enclosed by Beeley Wood, always climbing the 1 in 132/120 gradient. It comes as no surprise to hear that in steam days

banking engines were often needed all the way to Dunford Bridge. The woodland comes to an end after about a mile and the Silica & Firebrick works on our left, with an abandoned incline to old workings passing over us, heralds the approach to Oughty Bridge station, serving the village of Oughtibridge. Typically in this part of the world, the railway spelling is often different to the local spelling. We see little of the Silica works internal railway as we enter a cutting to pass under Oughtibridge Lane and through the station where a C13 4-4-2 tank is on a stopping service from Penistone. After the station, a connection from the Silica works comes in after crossing Oughtibridge Lane on the level, running alongside Station Lane and through the small goods yard. On the right is another large rail connected works.

As we re-enter woodland, a single line drops away from us to the left, travelling for three quarters of a mile through the trees and over the river to Dixon's paper mill on the river bank. We are on a short stretch of six-track railway with two goods loops on either side of us but once back on double track the trees close in and we start the journey through three miles of Wharncliffe Wood. It is punctuated only by a clearing about half way along where there are more loops and refuge sidings along with the like-named signal box. Just before the box, on the right, is an abandoned loading dock to which until about 15 years ago a rope-worked incline descended from Broad Stone quarry some 800ft above where there was a winding engine and lines to the various quarry faces. Earthworks on our left signify a light railway which until 1929 ran to the construction site of Broomhead and Moor Hall reservoirs, descending from here by a 1 in 26 zig-zag. It opened in 1914 and it is fair to say that at that point railways in the Sheffield area were at their fullest extent.

We are now on a four-track stretch and a long siding follows on the left. While not out of the woods yet we begin our approach to

With Wadsley Bridge behind it, B1 4-6-0 No. 61186 coasts downgrade over Herries Road bridge at the head of an early 1950s class B stopping train. *Tom Greaves*

Deepcar. The siding is crossed on the level by a line running into the General Refractories works as it continues behind Deepcar station before disappearing into the exchange sidings with the Stocksbridge Railway. Opened in April 1877 to exclusively serve Samuel Fox & Co's Stocksbridge ironworks, it is run as a railway company in its own right. On its way to the works, just under two miles away, it crosses the Don gorge by means of a 56ft-high viaduct consisting of an iron superstructure on stone piers. Until 1931 it carried passengers between Stocksbridge and Deepcar station - at their own risk. Between 1898 and 1912 an extension for Sheffield Corporation ran a further three miles to assist the building of Langsett Reservoir, completed in 1904.

From Deepcar we re-enter woodland until two miles further on we pass recently closed Wortley station. Then we trace a sweeping left hand curve with more woods on our left until we reach Thurgoland signal box where a siding curves sharply to the right. This was the Thurgoland Coal Branch, opened by the SA&MR in November 1847 and closed as long ago as 1875 but still shown on our 1906 Ordnance Survey map. The branch writhed its way two miles up the hillside to serve coal pits on Hollin Moor, beyond Thurgoland village. The first pits were encountered on Toad Hole Hill, just beyond the village; here were two loops, one after the other. The branch ended with another loop and a loading dock, presumably where small loads of coal from the various small pits were brought together.

Next is the twin-bore 350yd Thurgoland Tunnel. Until electrification it was a double track tunnel but with insufficient clearance for the two lines and overhead wires it was used for the Up line only and a new bore made for the Down line which we are now passing through. Emerging from the tunnel, we cross the River Don and enter a typical Pennine rural landscape. After passing Blackmoor Crossing and Oxspring we reach Willey Bridge Junction where the lines start to fan out. At Barnsley Junction we are met by the line from Wath and Barnsley coming in from the

right and, beyond it, Barnsley Junction sorting yard. On our left, between the yard and Huddersfield Junction, are more sidings, a turntable, and the David Brown steel works and its railway connections. We pass Huddersfield Junction where the former Lancashire & Yorkshire Railway line to Huddersfield, opened 1850, curves away to the right through its own platforms before we enter the main GC side of Penistone station. Penistone literally is the nerve centre for the MSW electrified lines for here is the electric power control for the whole system as well as the meeting point for railways feeding into it, and it is the base for the overhead line maintenance teams. Historically it is significant because in the 1860s a Bessemer steel plant was established here for the manufacture of rails.

There is some debate as to whether our engine can get water at Dunford Bridge since electrification. No-one is sure so rather than risk it, 40538 is topped up here. That done we press on, passing the small Penistone goods yard on our left as we return to typical Pennine surroundings. After Thurlstone signal box we are on a three-track railway with an extra running line on the left(Down) side which comes to an end at Bullhouse crossing where we cross the Manchester Road and pass Bullhouse Colliery. About a mile and a half on is closed Hazlehead Bridge station. There are a few sidings and loops along with an industrial line going away in a trailing direction on our right. Dating from the 1860s, this line runs to the Hepworth Iron company's pipe and tile works, Crowedge Colliery and Sledbrook Colliery situated at a 1000ft altitude. The branch includes a 1 in 23/25 gradient and is well known both for its quarter-mile tunnel alongside Mucky Lane and the attractive 0-6-0 tank engine that works it. A firebrick works is on the left from which a tramway to a ganister pit passes under our line.

At Dunford Bridge East signal box a line veers away to our right into the extensive sidings where trains from Lancashire were until recently remarshalled into trains bound for destinations in the east. We come to rest at Dunford Bridge's new station serving the

Before the full completion of electrification, B1 No. 61159 makes a smoky start from Penistone with the 7.31am Leicester-Manchester at 10.10am. EM1 Bo-Bo electric No. 26048 bides its time in the siding. *Tom Greaves*

remotest of communities - just a handful of houses and a pub, the trackless old station on our right being on the abandoned line to the old tunnels. The eastern portal of the new Woodhead Tunnel is ahead of us, 1000ft above sea level. No longer a black hole in a hill - it is illuminated by electric lights throughout, but this is as far as we go - steam engines are now banned from running through the tunnel under their own power. What a contrast to the old tunnel which had to be the nearest earthly thing to Hell for all who worked through or in it. As if this black hole permanently filled with suffocating smoke wasn't bad enough, a signal box was installed half way through in 1899 in an effort to improve line capacity. It had to be reached via a manhole and only lasted 10 years because few men could be found to work it.

With 40538 propelling again we run straight back to Woodburn Junction and curve left onto the Rotherham line, the section from here to Meadow Hall being opened in 1864 by the South Yorkshire Railway. Curving round in a cutting, we reach Attercliffe Junction and the curve from Darnall, opened in August 1873.

We continue in the cutting until crossing over the Sheffield & Tinsley Canal to pass the site of Attercliffe station, closed in 1927. On the opposite bank is Darnall steel works with an internal railway not connected to the main line. The canal continues alongside, beyond a group of sidings before closing in on our right while Brown Bayley's steel works looms on the left.

We have now descended into the heavily industrialized zone of the Lower Don Valley and are again bordered by foundries, steel plants and heavy engineering works. Once past Brown Bayley's, we approach Broughton Lane station, now threatened with closure. Approaching the station more industrial sidings curve away left. After the station we pass Broughton Lane sidings and the goods station down below on the left.

After T. W. Ward's Carbrook rolling mills and the works of

Tinsley Wire Industries, we pass under the Sheffield District Railway and then alongside the huge dark sheds of the many steel mills and engineering works crammed into the Meadow Hall area between us and the Midland line. Much of what we see is the Imperial Steel Works of Edgar Allen & Co, well known for track products. Unlike the Midland, we have rail connections wandering into narrow labyrinths between the various works buildings.

As we pass under the wide Sheffield Road bridge is Tinsley station, closed 1951, and its small local goods yard. At Tinsley Junction we take the original South Yorkshire line over the River Don while today's main route to Rotherham, also crossing the river, continues right. That line was opened as far as Rotherham in August 1868 and on to Mexborough in 1871, thus giving the MS&L a direct route between Sheffield Victoria and Doncaster.

Lines run from Tinsley Junction along the opposite bank of the river all the way round to sidings on the far side of the East Hecla works. The view is quickly blocked by Wincobank Rolling Mills as we come to Tinsley West Junction and the curve from East Junction, opened in July 1875 so that coal trains could run direct between Barnsley and Rotherham. A connection leads from this curve into the Blackburn Meadows sewerage works. Blackburn Meadows power station, which will have its own rail connections from the same spot, is under construction.

Passing under the Sheffield & Rotherham line, we part company with the River Don and now follow the Blackburn Valley, named after Blackburn Brook, a Don tributary. The Yorkshire Engine Company's works is on our left and then we come to Meadow Hall Junction. Here we join the South Yorkshire Railway's original Barnsley line along which its trains ran between Wicker and Barnsley or Doncaster. When the line to Woodburn Junction opened they were rerouted to Victoria and the Meadow Hall-Blackburn Valley section became just a connecting spur for goods.

The young fireman on a named B1 rendered anonymous by grime and steam, breaks up the coal during a pause at Tinsley Junction in the early 1960s. The South Yorkshire line to Barnsley goes straight ahead and the Rotherham line to the right, while the sidings on the left go into the mass of works covering the Meadow Hall area. *Tom Greaves*

It was just as well the SYR made this switch because its relations with the Midland had taken a turn for the worse. The SYR didn't bother with such minor details as Acts of Parliament when building its lines, believing them to be a tiresome burden. It laid its line under the Midland here by means of an existing underbridge. Taking exception, the Midland tore up the rails. The South Yorkshire put them back, and the Midland removed them again but even without an Act of Parliament the SY could prove its right of way. This was just one of a number of issues which would breed mistrust between the Midland and MS&L camps and their successors until nationalisation in 1948 - and knowing that old attitudes die hard, probably for some years after.

Continuing, we pass more engineering plants, such as the Arthur Lee & Sons Trubrite Steel Works and another British Acheson Electrode Works, until reaching Grange Lane. From just beyond the station, a single line opened in 1875 trails back and up the hillside, behind a housing estate and in front of Barber Wood to curve in a northerly direction to Grange Colliery, a mile and three quarters away at wistfully-named Dropping Well, Kimberworth.

With 40538 leading, we now run direct to Killamarsh West via Darnall, Woodhouse and Beighton, calling only at Tinsley for water, a spot where many freights are booked to top-up. Reversing at Killamarsh, our coach is again propelled as we head north along the Old Road. Approaching Beighton Junction again, a line comes down on the right in the direction we are travelling. This is the former Lancashire, Derbyshire & East Coast Railway, a company with grand aspirations. Its aim was to link deep water ports on the Lincolnshire coast and at Warrington. In the event it got no further than Lincoln in the east and Chesterfield in the west but is nevertheless an important freight route, especially for coal. The LD&EC also aimed to enter Sheffield but a branch from Langwith

Junction to the MS&L's Beighton-Annesley line at Killamarsh was the nearest it got, at least on its own.

In the fork between the Old Road and the line from Woodhouse are Beighton wagon shops and on our right Killamarsh Branch Sidings. Immediately after, we cross the River Rother and sidings go into an artificial stone works before the North Staveley Curve goes away right and up to Brookhouse Colliery and coke ovens. There it would take two reversals through sidings to access the Retford line at North Staveley Junction.

Above us on the right, just before we pass under the Retford line is Beighton Colliery which is connected by sidings to Brookhouse. After the intersection is Woodhouse Mill Down Yard on our left, consisting of something like 16 through roads and nine dead ends. Next on our left is the Rothervale Joinery Works who's internal system includes a wagon turntable. Passing closed Woodhouse Mill station, we notice a sewerage works on the left with an extensive 2ft gauge railway.

We are now in a wild landscape of marshes, scrub and spoil heaps but before long, on our left, are Treeton Sidings from which a branch leads to an extensive and tangled industrial railway system within the smoking mass of Orgreave Colliery, coke and chemical works. Closed Treeton station follows and then, as we traverse a cutting, Treeton Junction. Over the top passes the Treeton Colliery Railway linking Treeton Colliery, on our right, to the Orgreave complex and, in effect, forming a through line to the GC at Orgreaves. Until the 1930s it carried miners' trains from Sheffield Victoria. Treeton Colliery also has a connection to the Old Road just beyond the junction but we are taking the left turnout onto the Sheffield District Railway.

Several companies had sought access to Sheffield during the late 19th century, among them the Great Eastern Railway which one

WD 2-8-0 No. 90647 comes off the Silverwood branch and on to the South Yorkshire Rotherham-Mexborough line at Thrybergh Junction. The Thrybergh bridge is in the left background and Roundwood rolling mills in the right distance. *Tom Greaves*

might consider to be somewhat remote from this industrial area in all aspects, its normal business being rural lines in East Anglia and London commuters. However, the GER had come as close as Lincoln via its joint line with the Great Northern and was eyeing profitable coal and steel hauls to London via this route - in direct competition with the Midland and the GC. The LD&EC could provide the GE with a route from Lincoln and so the GE invested heavily in it while proposing an extension from Killamarsh to Attercliffe. Upon seeing this, the Midland proposed a line of its own from Treeton to Brightside but after negotiations the competing parties agreed to combine their efforts and follow the Midland's route. In return, the Midland granted the GE and LD&EC running powers along its own lines from Beighton to Treeton, Brightside to Grimesthorpe, and for passenger trains to Pond Street station. Thus, the Sheffield District Railway - the last main line to enter Sheffield - was opened in May 1900 along with the LD&EC's connection to the Old Road at Beighton. Within seven years the LD&EC was taken over by the GC which gained running powers over the District Railway as a result, while the Great Northern also acquired running powers for freight. Consequently, we are now on a line that ended up being shared by several rivals, but despite this it was little use to any of them and became something of a sleeping white elephant.

Curving round, we pass a rail-connected spoil tip on our right with an internal railway and engine shed which appears disused. Crossing the River Rother on a nine-arch viaduct we then pass Catcliffe station, closed to passengers in 1939, before entering a deep cutting followed by the 80-yard Tinsley Wood Tunnel. After a stretch of open country, a single track opened by the SDR in 1903 to Tinsley Park Colliery curves left while there are eight sidings leading to an opencast coal loading point. Lines on the right lead to Firth Vickers Shepcote Lane stainless steel mills.

Compared to other lines in Sheffield, the quantity of railway

along here is sparse and we are now on another stretch of double track uninterrupted by sidings or works connections. Then, we pass over the Sheffield & Tinsley Canal, the GC Sheffield-Rotherham line, and Sheffield Road - and everything changes. First is West Tinsley station, also closed in 1939, but coming up from the left, are connections from Tinsley Wire and Firth Vickers Staybrite works. One the right is West Tinsley goods yard from which connections descend to Edgar Allen's works with its Tramway & Machinery department. Passing over Vulcan Road, we encounter more sidings and a line dropping to Cooper & Turner's rivet & brass works. On the right a single track descends at 1 in 40 to follow the River Don into the Meadow Hall complex with the Brightside steel works its first customer. It continues alongside the Don, serving other plants until it reaches the sidings alongside Hadfields' East Hecla works. A single track passing beneath us leads to another part of the Brightside Works on our left.

Now we cross the River Don and Meadow Hall Road by a viaduct consisting of six 30ft spans, a 100ft lattice girder bridge and an 80ft plate girder section to reach Brightside Station Junction. Passing Grimesthorpe loco shed again, we swing to the left. A connection on the left goes into Attercliffe Steel Works and then we cross the River Don and enter Attercliffe goods yard, the LD&EC's own Sheffield terminus.

Our marathon over, we alight feeling that we have just witnessed one of the most complex railway systems and greatest concentrations of industry anywhere, with what seems to be steel or heavy engineering works, collieries and coking plants and all kinds of other industries one after the other with barely a break between them.

It's worth recounting here that although Sheffield's railways were dominated by the Midland and Great Central, other companies gained access to the city and its industrial wealth via running powers and agreements. The Great Northern, the London

Class O4/8 2-8-0 No. 63776 pounds away from Killamarsh and up the LD&EC line with a long train of empties on Saturday 24th November 1962. The train is thought to be the 8.40am Greasborough Road-Warsop Junction. *Robert Anderson*

& North Western, the Great Eastern and the Lancashire, Derbyshire & East Coast have already been mentioned. Others running their trains into Sheffield were the Lancashire & Yorkshire which came from Huddersfield and Bradford via Penistone, the North Eastern Railway with services from York and Hull, and the Hull & Barnsley Railway via Cudworth and the North Midland line. In 1922 the NER took over the Hull & Barnsley and the LNWR took over the Lancashire & Yorkshire in readiness for a big shake-up when the various companies were merged into just four. On 1st January 1923, the Great Central combined with the Great Northern, Great Eastern, North Eastern and others to form the London & North Eastern Railway. The Midland was merged with the London & North Western and others to form the London Midland & Scottish. They in turn were nationalised from 1st January 1948 to form one organisation, British Railways, although that did not prevent much of the railway, especially around Sheffield, still being operated along pre-grouping lines. In the 1990s the railways were de-nationalised and put in the hands of private companies with Railtrack(since replaced by Network Rail) responsible for the infrastructure and control of operations, and a myriad of private train operators.

Passenger services

Sheffield may have started at the end of a branch line but by the end of the 1860s it had gained direct services to two London stations - King's Cross and Euston Square(St. Pancras from 1868) and also to Leeds, Bradford, Derby, Birmingham, York,

Manchester, Huddersfield, Lincoln, Grimsby, Cleethorpes, Barnsley, Doncaster and the North East. In 1849 the Midland had begun a service between Wicker and Doncaster using the North Midland line to Swinton and a curve down to the South Yorkshire Railway's new line from Barnsley. From 1851 the GNR was running Bridgehouses(and then Victoria)-King's Cross through carriages by way of Lincoln. The King's Cross via Retford route, opened up in 1852, would at various times carry Sheffield's fastest London service until the late 1960s; and from 1857 the GN was running King's Cross-Manchester "flyers" via this route.

These were tentative beginnings but the 1870s brought a real step change. The new Midland line to the south and the station in Pond Street now put Sheffield on a direct express route between London, the South, the Midlands and the North. Passenger trains until then using the Old Road were transferred to the new line through Sheffield - but not all. Just to keep on needling Sheffield, a few of the prime expresses continued to avoid the city and passengers had to change at Rotherham Masborough for decades to come. Opening of the Settle & Carlisle in 1876 added Scotland to the route. Completion of the Swinton & Knottingley Joint line by the Midland and North Eastern railways in 1879 enabled more direct services between Sheffield, York and the North East.

By 1883 the GN's two King's-Cross Manchester trains were covering the London-Sheffield stretch in 3 hours 25 minutes, and that with a stop to exchange GN and MSL locos at Grantham. The following year, the 2pm from Manchester, consisting of five or six 6-wheelers including a Bradford coach, became the fastest train in Britain and one of the fastest in the world by averaging 54mph from Grantham to London behind a GN loco. Between Sheffield and Grantham the MS&L locos weren't much slower, averaging 51mph. By the 1890s there were five or six King's Cross-Manchester trains each way on weekdays and Sheffield-King's Cross journey times were down to 3 hours 9 mins.

By the end of the century, Sheffield also had services to Barnsley by two routes - the MS&L from Victoria and the Midland from Pond Street. Sheffield's first ever passenger service from Rotherham Westgate had been extended through to Chinley and Manchester Central upon opening of the Hope Valley line in 1894.

Then, in 1899, came the opening of the Great Central main line to Nottingham, Leicester, Rugby and London Marylebone. It triggered a contest between three companies for the fastest Sheffield-London time. The Great Central offered a best time of 2 hours 57 min., just clipping the Midland's best of 3 hours. By 1905 the GN's 6.5pm Kings Cross-Manchester was running to Sheffield in 2 hours 50 min., a record time which would hold until 1958. The GC matched this with the same time by its non-stop 3.25pm from Marylebone. Both companies called their trains "The Sheffield Special." The Midland wasn't far behind with a best time of 2 hours 59 min. At this point, Sheffield could not say it was not well served by London trains. But after a spell as fastest to London, the GN service was withdrawn during the first world war and not reinstated afterwards.

The GC brought new long-distance cross-country services through links to the South West and south coast via Woodford, Banbury and Oxford. It soon ran Newcastle-Bournemouth, Manchester-Dover, Scarborough-Southampton Docks, Liverpool-Yarmouth and West Yorkshire-Bristol trains or through carriages, along with Liverpool and Manchester-Grimsby and Harwich boat trains, the latter in partnership with the Great Eastern.

Expresses or through carriages were also run between Bradford Exchange, Huddersfield and Marylebone in association with the Lancashire & Yorkshire who worked the through trains between Bradford and Sheffield.

Besides its St.Pancras-Sheffield-Leeds-Bradford-Glasgow-Edinburgh trunk expresses, now including sleeping car trains, the Midland was running services between Bristol, Birmingham, Derby, Sheffield, and York and Newcastle in partnership with the NER. There were also St. Pancras-Stranraer and Heysham boat trains along with through carriages to Halifax, Bradford Exchange and Harrogate. For a time in the early 20th century the Midland also had a Manchester-Harwich boat train by means of through carriages on a Lincoln express which travelled from Pond Street via the District Railway and the LD&EC. From Lincoln the carriages were combined with the GC portion and taken forward by the Great Eastern.

The Hull & Barnsley entered the scene in 1905, courtesy of the Midland, when it began running expresses from Hull Cannon Street beyond its Cudworth terminus and along the North Midland to Pond Street. Alas, the H&B's elegant Stirling 4-4-0s were not seen at Pond Street for long as the service was a victim of world war one cuts when it retreated permanently back to Cudworth.

In summer 1922, just months before the Midland and the Great Central became opposing parts of the "Big Four," Sheffield was served by something like 370 passenger trains each weekday, just under 200 either starting, terminating or calling at the Midland station, and around 170 at Victoria.

Nevertheless, they were not at the level of just 10 years earlier. Some axed during the first world war had not resumed. There were now no King's Cross expresses, nor was there a fast early morning express to London. The Midland's 7.5am to St. Pancras offered the best morning service, taking 3 hours 40 min., while the first direct London train from Victoria was the 9.35am "Luncheon

In this early 1950s view, Stanier Class 5 4-6-0 No. 45260 is about to pass its home shed at Millhouses while heading along the Up Local line with a Hope Valley service. The lines in the foreground and the underpass at the southern exit from Sheffield were added when the route was widened at the start of the 20th century. The southern exit from Sheffield is more residential in nature. *Tom Greaves*

Corridor" express originating from Manchester London Road and due in Marylebone at 1.13pm. The Midland's fastest London train was the 8.56am from Sheffield "Bradford & Leeds Express" which reached the capital in 3 hours 14 min. Next was the 10.40am 'Scotch Express' from Edinburgh, taking just three and a quarter hours. Some other Midland expresses took between 3 hours 15 and 3 hours 35 min. But the Great Central's 3.20pm "Restaurant Corridor Express" from Marylebone(through carriages to Halifax) was the fastest overall, taking only 3 hours 6 min. Other GC expresses were scheduled to take between 3 hours 13 and 3 hours 53 min. These times were slower than the pre-war schedules achieved by the GN and the GC especially, and Sheffield might again feel justifiably unhappy with its London services.

On the North East-South West route, 11 northbound expresses and seven southbound connected such places as Newcastle, Bradford, Leeds, Sheffield, Birmingham, Gloucester, Bristol, Bournemouth and Paignton. As with London services, a few took the Old Road and missed Sheffield.

Through carriage portions featured strongly in those days with some complex workings. One example was the 7.20am Bradford Exchange and Halifax-St Pancras which arrived at 8.42 conveying a Bristol portion. Eight minutes later the 7.20am Bradford Market Street-St. Pancras arrived with a Heysham-London portion. The 7.20 from Bradford Exchange departed at 8.56 with the Heysham portion but minus the Bristol portion while the 7.20 from Bradford Market Street left at 9.2 for London via Melton Mowbray. At 9.24 the 7.44am Bradford Market Street-Bristol arrived with a Bournemouth portion and left at 9.30 without the Bournemouth portion but with the Halifax-Bristol portion. The Bournemouth portion then went forward as the 9.46 from Sheffield, picking up through carriages from Lincoln and Nottingham at Derby.

The Hope Valley line enjoyed a good weekday service of 13 trains each way being a mix of stopping trains and expresses between Rotherham Westgate or Sheffield and Manchester Central. There was also a summer Sheffield-Llandudno express each way and a handful of peak hour or Saturday stopping trains to/from Hope, Edale or Chinley.

The Midland ran three weekday trains each way between Sheffield and Doncaster via Swinton. Six Sheffield-York trains were run each way via the S&K plus a couple to Pontefract and back. The Barnsley service was graced with 12 trains from Sheffield and 11 from Barnsley plus an extra each way on Saturdays. Nine local trains a day ran direct from Chesterfield to Sheffield and six the other way though the two were also connected by longer-distance trains. The Sheffield-Chesterfield service via Holmes, Treeton, Woodhouse Mill and Eckington comprised the 8.20am, 12.55pm, 5.40pm, and 10.48pm Saturday, from Sheffield with six arrivals from Chesterfield from 9.31am to 10.25pm. Besides these were the 11.42am, 7.34pm and 9.25pm from Sheffield and the 5.35am arrival which ran via the District Railway. The joint service with the Great Central via Catcliffe and the LD&EC saw trains from Pond Street to Mansfield at 9.45am, 3.15 and 6.20 plus 11pm(Saturday) with trains from Mansfield due in Sheffield at 11.46am, 2.7(Saturday,) 5.54 and 8.25pm. There was also a 6.42am shuttle to West Tinsley and back.

On the GC side in summer 1922, despite the London extension, the original MS&L route still formed the backbone of the main line service with five through trains from Manchester London Road to Cleethorpes and four in the opposite direction on weekdays plus one Manchester Central-Cleethorpes and one Sheffield-Cleethorpes each way. Besides these were nine trains a day from Sheffield Victoria to Retford or Lincoln, and 11 from Lincoln or Retford. In addition were the Liverpool/Manchester-Harwich "Continental Boat Express" each way, and a summer service Manchester London Road-Yarmouth, the return train conveying Lowestoft to Liverpool through carriages.

Three Marylebone-Manchester and two Marylebone-Bradford expresses ran each way on the main line plus one Sheffield-Marylebone each way. These were augmented by various Liverpool/Manchester/Sheffield-Nottingham/Leicester trains.

GC cross-country services ran between Sheffield and Weston-super-Mare, Newcastle and Swansea, Portsmouth-Scarborough with through carriages from Southampton and to Edinburgh and Glasgow, plus Glasgow/Edinburgh-Southampton Docks and Penzance-Glasgow/Aberdeen sleepers. The 10.3pm York-Bristol missed Victoria by taking the Attercliffe-Darnall curve, Sheffield passengers having to change at Rotherham & Masborough(later Central.) Completing Victoria's range of expresses were three Hull-Liverpool Central trains each way.

The Rotherham line also saw five Sheffield-Doncaster trains each way, one to Cleethorpes, one to Hull and Cleethorpes dividing at Doncaster, two Sheffield-Hull and three Hull-Sheffield trains, one from Liverpool Central to Cleethorpes, plus a small number of Stainforth & Hatfield-Sheffield and Mexborough-Sheffield trains. The GC also ran three trains to York, one from York, and one from Scarborough. Local trains also ran between Sheffield, Chesterfield Central and Nottingham Victoria. The GC's Barnsley line saw nine trains each way(10 from Sheffield on Saturdays) including the 2.40pm from Barnsley and 9.38pm from Sheffield conveying a through carriage to/from Marylebone. Three stopping trains ran from Victoria to Wortley, five to Penistone and four to Manchester with six from Manchester and six from Penistone.

With the Grouping out of the way and the hangover from war receding, the new companies confidently strode forward into what has often been described as the "Golden Age" of rail travel. In 1924, the LNER reinstated a King's Cross service - The Sheffield Pullman - which ran via Nottingham. A commercial flop, it was rerouted via Retford and extended to/from Manchester within a matter of weeks. The return journey, the 6.5pm non-stop from Victoria with five coaches was booked to take 2 hours 57 min. - the best London time since 1914. The fastest GC time was 3 hours 6 min. and the Midland 3 hours 7 min. Still not a success, the Pullman was withdrawn in September 1925.

The 1920s saw the LMS name its principal "Scotch Expresses" The Thames-Clyde Express and The Thames-Forth Express, although the northbound Thames-Clyde brought little cudos to Sheffield as it went via the Old Road. It also inaugurated The Devonian between Bradford and Paignton and, in summer, Kingswear. It launched The Yorkshireman, the 9.10am Bradford Exchange-St. Pancras and 4.55pm return and in 1925 began a new fast Bradford-St. Pancras express each way. In 1937 a Jubilee-hauled St. Pancras-Sheffield was booked for 2 hours 52 min. but as it couldn't keep time it was decelerated to 3 hours 5 min.

On the GC, B17 4-6-0s began working principal expresses during the 1920s including the Harwich boat trains. Then in 1938 the GC almost achieved motive power parity with the East Coast main line when A1 Pacifics and V2 2-6-2s replaced the B17s on the heaviest and most important London trains.

But war loomed again and from 1939 there was no place for glamourous expresses as movement of troops and supplies took precedence. The King's Cross trains were among the casualties, as was the District Railway's remaining passenger service - consisting of a LMS 2P 4-4-0 and two LNER coaches. It was withdrawn on 11th September 1939, never to be reinstated except for a short spell in the severe 1947 winter when snow blocked local roads. One prime express to keep running was the Thames-Clyde, minus such peace-time frivolity as its name.

As we enter the era which Railway Memories books are mainly about, we find a railway system battered and completely worn out by six years of war. It took well over a decade for passenger services to recover to anything even approaching their pre-war standards, a situation aggravated by ongoing shortages of coal, materials and staff and a huge backlog of maintenance work.

The LMS reinstated The Thames-Forth Express in 1945 but it was much slower than pre-war. In 1947 the popular pre-war 7.30am "Breakfast Car Special" from Victoria to Marylebone was revived and accelerated to 3 hours 35min. to be the fastest train to London by any route(remember 2 hour 50min. before the first world war.) It was named The Master Cutler and carried a Sheffield stainless steel headboard presented by the Master of the Company of Cutlers. The occasion marked the beginning of a Sheffield icon, a train that was the city's own and a name still carried by a St. Pancras service in 2013. Even so, there was often nothing better than a B1 4-6-0 to work this 9-coach express and so it had to be decelerated by 12 minutes just to keep time.

It must be said that in the British Railways era especially, the GC main line was plagued by inadequate motive power, whether it be under-powered locomotives or locomotives in poor condition. This applied equally to The South Yorkshireman introduced by BR on 31st May 1948 as a revival of the pre-war 10am Bradford-Marylebone express. It was heavily-loaded and although relatively slow taking 4 hours 3 min., it was so popular that a relief was often run - yet it too was usually in the charge of a B1. In 1949 BR

restored the Thames-Clyde name and then, in 1951, Pacifics returned to work the best GC expresses - at least for a time.

The railways were now under one organisation and one of the first acts by British Railways was to rename the ex-LMS station at Sheffield City in 1950, but nine months later it was again renamed Sheffield Midland. Rationalisation of duplicating services was next, especially since many passengers had been lost to more convenient buses. The Sheffield Victoria-Barnsley service - reduced to just two trains from Victoria and three from Barnsley by 1946 - was axed on 7th December 1953, although freight and special traffic continued. The following summer, the Sheffield-Chesterfield local service via the Old Road was withdrawn Treeton, Woodhouse Mill and Killamarsh West stations having already closed. However, the loss was probably over-shadowed by what happened on 20th September. On that day the Manchester-Sheffield electrification was inaugurated and all passenger trains between Victoria and Manchester London Road became electrically-hauled. Billed as Britain's first all-electric main line, it gave Sheffield the most advanced inter-city service in the country. In the first six weeks passenger numbers leapt by 37 per cent and by 1956, when certain speed restrictions had been lifted, the Manchester-Sheffield journey time was down to just 47 minutes. The Midland line was then speeded up with some major journey time reductions as the post-war hangover began to lift, and in 1957 the Thames-Forth was accelerated and renamed The Waverley.

In 1958 came a reorganisation which would profoundly affect Sheffield's main line services. Since nationalisation, operational responsibility for the whole of the GC main line had remained with the LNER's successor, BR's Eastern Region. But in 1958 everything west of Dunford Bridge and south of Pilsley, near Chesterfield, was transferred to the London Midland Region, successor to the LMS. The LM now found itself with two competing routes to London and so the eight-year painful rundown

Stanier Class 5 4-6-0 No. 44912, of Low Moor shed, coasts down past Bridgehouses on the approach to Sheffield Victoria with The South Yorkshireman in 1951. The chances are a B1 would be waiting to take the train forward to Marylebone. *Alan Ashley*
There used to be a tunnel hereabouts but it was opened out and the lines widened in 1913.

The north end of Sheffield(Midland) in the late 1940s could still offer a glimpse of the 1920s when Midland Railway expresses were double headed by small engines, usually 4-4-0s. Midland Railway Johnson 2P 4-4-0, No. 553 of the LMS, is seen piloting more modern power in the form of a Stanier Class 5 4-6-0 at the head of a St. Pancras-Leeds express. *Tom Greaves*

of the GC in favour of the Midland began. With immediate effect the Eastern switched The Master Cutler to its own 161.2-mile King's Cross route via Retford. The Up train left Sheffield at 7.20am and arrived King's Cross at 10.5am, the Down train leaving King's Cross at 7.20pm to arrive Victoria at 10.5pm. It brought an instant 52 minute cut in journey time compared to the 164.7-mile journey to Marylebone and was 28 minutes faster than the 158.5-mile Midland route's equivilant, the 7.5am to St. Pancras. Not only that, the Cutler was now a 6-coach Pullman train hauled by the first diesels on the East Coast main line. So prestigious was it, that London's Hornsey depot, where the new English Electric Type 4s were based, was ordered to give the Cutler top priority for diesel power over anything else. To make full use of the loco and stock, the Pullmans also ran from King's Cross to Sheffield and back during the day. The Sheffield-London time was cut to 2 hours 40min. in 1963 when English Electric Type 3s replaced the overweight Type 4s. The Sheffield Pullmans became a proving ground for various diesel types such as uprated Brush Type 2s(temporarily Type 3 or 4) which performed well, and manufacturers' prototypes such as Brush *Falcon* and the BRCW/AEI/Sulzer *Lion*.

In summer 1959 Sheffield Midland saw a total of just under 160 trains on Mondays to Fridays. Most prolific were the Thames-Clyde Express(10.15am St. Pancras-Glasgow St. Enoch calling Sheffield 1.23-30pm and 9.20am Glasgow-St. Pancras calling 3.36-42pm,) The Waverley(9.15am St. Pancras-Edinburgh calling at Sheffield 12.28-33pm and 10.5am Edinburgh-St. Pancras calling 4.37-43pm/4.50-56 on Sats) and The Devonian(10.15am Bradford Forster Square-Paignton calling Sheffield 11.54am-12 noon - via Old Road on Sats - and 9.15am Paignton-Bradford calling 4.43-54pm - from Kingswear and calling Sheffield 5.54-51 on Sats.) Apart from a 9am summer relief to the Thames-Clyde from Glasgow on Mondays and Fridays(Sheffield 3.24-30pm,) the Waverley and Thames-Clyde were the only Monday-Friday daytime expresses running throughout between St. Pancras and Scotland. But there were sleeper trains, the 9pm St. Pancras-Edinburgh(Sheffield at 12.52-1am,) the 9.15pm St. Pancras-

Glasgow(Sheffield 1.22-32am,) the 9.5pm Glasgow-St. Pancras (Sheffield 3.50-56am/3.45-51 on Mondays,) and the 9.55pm Edinburgh-St. Pancras(Sheffield 4.57-5.3am.) One other sleeper was the 11.50pm St. Pancras-Leeds calling Sheffield at 4.25-32am. Four trains from St. Pancras to Leeds and Bradford with five the other way, and three St. Pancras-Sheffield each way made up a total of nine Down and 10 Up daytime expresses between Sheffield and St. Pancras. The first train to London was the 7.5am from Sheffield, booked to take 3 hours 13 min., although the fastest was the 8.33am departure, timed for 3 hours 7 min. The fastest from London was the Thames-Clyde in 3 hours 8 min. with the 5.5pm St. Pancras-Bradford taking in 3 hours 12min.

Newcastle and West Yorkshire-Bristol trains were the mainstay of the express service on the North East-South West route. There were three Newcastle, one York and three Bradford Forster Square to Bristol trains with two from Bristol to Newcastle, three to Sheffield, one to Forster Square, one each way between Newcastle and Birmingham, one from Birmingham to Bradford, one from Newcastle to Cardiff, one from Sheffield to Worcester, one from Worcester to York, one each way between Bradford and Paignton, and one each from Sheffield to Bournemouth West and Gloucester. Semi-fast and stopping trains ran between various points along the Bradford-Leeds-Cudworth-Sheffield-Derby/Nottingham corridor.

Three ran from Chesterfield Midland while Nottingham and Derby trains covered the local service the other way. Six weekday locals came from York via Pontefract Baghill and five plus one summer dated went to York; there was one Sheffield Midland-Hull each way via Swinton, plus a Friday evening train to Hull which formed an overnight Hull-Paignton summer dated service.

On the Hope Valley were seven Sheffield-Chinley stopping trains with six from Chinley, one Sheffield-Manchester Central each way(one extra from Sheffield on Sats,) one train from Stockport Tiviot Dale and a fast train from Manchester each evening, plus one Monday-Friday Rotherham Masborough to Manchester Central and one Chinley to Masborough - a remnant of the old Rotherham Westgate service. Nearly as many trains were running

The Thames-Clyde Express was arguably the most celebrated train on the Midland main line.
The Up train is seen near Dore & Totley in the mid-1950s hauled by well groomed Holbeck Jubilee No. 45659 *Drake*.
Tom Greaves

on Sundays in the summer. The most lavish Midland lines local service was, not surprisingly, between Sheffield and Barnsley Court House. It consisted of 20 weekday trains from Sheffield and 21 from Barnsley with extras on Saturdays - entirely operated by diesel multiple units which had entered service across the area over the previous 12 months. Some York and Cudworth services were also DMUs by this time.

Victoria station and the GC lines saw just over 120 passenger trains on Mondays to Fridays in summer 1959. Undoubtedly the most important of these and of all Sheffield's trains were the Pullmans. The Master Cutler left Victoria at 7.20am and King's Cross at 7.20pm, both diesel-hauled with a booked journey time of 2 hours 45 minutes. The Pullman cars returned to Sheffield on the 11.20am from London and returned to King's Cross at 3.20pm, these latter trains running to more leisurely timings. At the time, the Hornsey-based English Electric Type 4s were very intensively diagrammed, and during its overnight layover in Sheffield the Cutler's loco was used on freight.

Sheffield still had five daytime expresses to Marylebone. On Mondays to Fridays they left Victoria at 7.50am, 9.31am(8.30 ex-Manchester London Road - soon to be renamed Piccadilly,) 11.36(The South Yorkshireman,) 3.11pm(2.10 ex-Manchester,) and 5.3pm(4.5 ex-Manchester.) Northbound London expresses arrived at 2.20pm(10am Marylebone-Manchester,) 4.27pm(12.15 Marylebone-Manchester,) 7.20pm (3.20 Marylebone-Manchester,) 8.42pm (4.50 Marylebone-Bradford South Yorkshireman,) and 10.1pm(6.18 ex-Marylebone.) Extras ran on Saturdays. Five more electric trains ran purely from Sheffield to Manchester and six from Manchester, some calling at Dunford Bridge and Woodhead. Connections were made at Penistone with Huddersfield trains. Supplementing these were odd Nottingham-Manchester London Road, Leicester-Manchester Central and London Road, and Sheffield-Leicester trains, plus the 10pm Marylebone-Liverpool Central and 9.30pm Liverpool-Marylebone. Weekday cross-country expresses had dwindled. The 8.35am Newcastle-Bournemouth reversed at Victoria to depart at 12.1pm, and the 11.16am Bournemouth-Newcastle arrived at 6pm. Of course, there were many more on summer Saturdays. The other cross-country

trains were the 6.40pm(starting Scarborough from 11th July,) and 10.22pm York-Swindon, 9.40pm Swindon-York, 7.30pm Swindon-Sheffield and a summer Friday 8.15am Swansea-Newcastle. Completing the principal services were the two Hull-Liverpool Central trains each way and the Liverpool-Harwich boat trains running via Retford and Lincoln: the 8am from Parkeston Quay, arriving Victoria at 12.54pm, and the 1.15pm from Liverpool Central, leaving Victoria at 3.30pm for Harwich Town.

Apart from Pullmans and boat trains, the Retford line carried three Manchester London Road to Cleethorpes trains(plus one extra to Grimsby early on Monday mornings,) seven Sheffield to Cleethorpes, and five Cleethorpes to Sheffield - one continuing to Manchester. Three ran Sheffield to Retford with the 8.52pm from Sheffield continuing to Gainsborough Central and forming the next morning's 7.8am from Gainsborough. Another three ran Retford to Sheffield, one continuing to Manchester. Five local trains a day ran from Victoria to Lincoln and seven from Lincoln. The summer timetable also advertised one mid-week Sheffield to Skegness at 10.20am, and a Manchester Central-Cambridge each way on Mondays, Fridays and Saturdays.

Besides the expresses already mentioned, the weekday passenger service over the Woodburn Junction-Rotherham Central line in summer 1959 consisted of four Sheffield to Doncaster trains and seven from Doncaster plus two Cleethorpes to Sheffield, three Hull-Sheffield each way, and one each to York via Doncaster and the S&K. The York-Swindon which came via Doncaster, was often heavily loaded and booked to attach an assisting engine at Rotherham when required for the gradients approaching Sheffield. There were also two through carriage workings to Leeds Central via Doncaster at 4.20 and 6.20am and one such working from Leeds arriving at 3.30am. Another, was the Fridays Only 6.28pm Doncaster-Liverpool Central, a portion which combined with the 4.12pm Hull-Liverpool at Victoria.

The remaining local services on the GC lines consisted of three Nottingham via Chesterfield trains each way plus three from Chesterfield (one extra on Sats) and one to Chesterfield, the 2.17pm to Nottingham direct, and the 8.46pm to Leicester and 6am Nottingham-Manchester London Road, both via Chesterfield.

The future must have looked very bright for Sheffield Victoria in 1954 when it hosted Britain's first all-electric inter-city service. Class EM2 Co-Co No. 27005 is in platform 4 having arrived with an express from Manchester London Road c1957. If a through service going further afield, it will be handing over to a steam loco. *Peter Cookson collection*

Penistone's local service to Barnsley and Doncaster had just been withdrawn. Diesel units were now appearing in numbers and the services they operated included some between Victoria and Lincoln, Cleethorpes, Retford, Doncaster and Hull, plus the weekday 10.20 to Skegness.

Summer Saturdays were an especially hectic time in Sheffield between the 1950s and 1970s and a look at the summer 1959 timetable illustrates the scale of Saturday traffic at a time when it was virtually at its peak. Universal car ownership and overseas package holidays were yet to make their mark, but the ability to afford two weeks annual holiday at the British seaside during July and August led to a mass movement of humanity every Saturday for just a few weeks as thousands began and ended their holidays on that one day of the week.

To cope with this surge in demand, around a hundred extra trains were booked to run between Sheffield and resorts all over Britain every summer Saturday, and they were fairly evenly divided between the Midland and GC systems. This number of trains includes overnight trains starting on a Friday but not unscheduled reliefs or privately-chartered excursions. Through Victoria were Manchester Central-Mablethorpe, Skegness and Yarmouth, Manchester London Road-Skegness and Cleethorpes, Chesterfield-Blackpool, Newcastle-Swansea, Bradford Exchange-Poole, and Blackpool-Cleethorpes trains. Originating in Sheffield were trains between Victoria and Boston, Yarmouth, Skegness, Portsmouth Harbour, Hastings, Clacton, Bridlington, Scarborough and Butlins' Filey Holiday Camp. On summer Saturdays the Newcastle-Bournemouth avoided Victoria by taking the Attercliffe-Darnall curve in both directions, an additional Victoria-Bournemouth train running in its place for Sheffield holidaymakers.

Some Skegness and Yarmouth trains travelled via the LD&EC between Killamarsh and Lincoln. A curiosity was the daily 5.45am anglers' special from Wadsley Bridge(closed to regular services from 15th June) to Woodhall Junction(between Lincoln and Boston) and return; it also ran on Sundays and was advertised in the public timetable. Among summer Saturday trains skirting the Sheffield area was a Tibshelf Town-Skegness each way via the Killamarsh-Waleswood curve. A Manchester-Scarborough ran via Penistone, Barnsley, Wath and the S&K.

Saturday extras through Midland station included trains between Newcastle and Paignton, Newcastle-Newquay, Newquay-York, Chesterfield-Bridlington, Derby-Scarborough, Filey-Derby, Bradford-Paignton, Teignmouth and Bournemouth West-Bradford, Bournemouth West-Leeds, and Derby-Glasgow. There were also Sheffield-Blackpool North, Morecambe, Newquay, Paignton, Weston-super-Mare, Bournemouth West, Skegness and Kingswear trains, and Sheffield-Blackpool Central, Bangor and Llandudno trains via the Hope Valley. Nottingham and Leicester-Blackpool trains also took the Hope Valley using the Dore South-West curve. Friday nights saw a St. Pancras-Glasgow relief each way along with Sheffield-Bournemouth West and Paignton, and Bradford and Hull-Paignton trains. More summer Saturday trains took the Old Road, including a Leicester London Road-Scarborough, a King's Norton-Scarborough, a Gloucester Eastgate-Filey Holiday Camp and a Nottingham-Morecambe. Despite a massive decline in summer Saturday traffic, some of these services would continue in similar form for the next 30 years with Sheffield-Skegness and Paignton-Newcastle trains being among the country's last loco-hauled summer Saturday extras. At 7.33am on summer Saturdays the 5.20am unadvertised Leicester-Craigendoran Creative Travel

Premier train of the North East-South West route was The Devonian between Bradford, Leeds and Paignton. Leeds Holbeck Jubilee No. 45569 *Tasmania* has charge of the Up train calling at Sheffield Midland at 12.5pm on Saturday 17th March 1962. *Robert Anderson*

Agents Conference charter left Midland station, returning at 9.10pm. Nowadays, the summer Saturday timetable is little different to that on weekdays.

With car ownership spreading fast by the end of the 1950s but with the motorway network in its infancy and long-distance driving still a challenge, BR capitalized by providing a service of car sleeper trains(later branded Motorail) to save motorists the long haul and these added to the rich tapestry of night-time extras passing through the area, mainly avoiding the Sheffield stations. In summer 1960 these were the 9.43pm Sunday and 9.35pm Wednesday Sutton Coldfield-Stirling, and 8.35pm Monday and Thursday night return; the 7.45pm Monday, Wednesday and Friday Marylebone-Glasgow and 6.38pm Monday, Wednesday and Saturday night return; the 7.45pm Tuesday, Thursday and Saturday Marylebone-Perth via the GC and York and its 5.8pm Tuesday, Thursday, Sunday night return; and the Friday 9.25pm Dover-Newcastle also via the GC. During the 1960s and 70s Sheffield had its own Motorail terminal served by a weekly Newton Abbot train. On top of these were the unadvertised "Starlight Specials" on Friday and Saturday nights - the 10.15pm (11.10 Sat) and 11pm high summer only(11.30 Sat) Marylebone to Glasgow and 8 and 8.25pm(high summer only) return; the Friday 9.35pm(when required) and 9.45pm and Saturday nights 9.50 (when required) and 9.40 Marylebone-Edinburgh via Attercliffe and York, and their Friday and Saturday night returns. The Marylebone-Glasgow trains had to be on the Midland north of Sheffield which necessitated a detour north of Nottingham via Langwith Junction and the LD&EC to the Old Road at Beighton.

Non-passenger overnights on the Midland included the 5.47pm Carlisle-Cricklewood milk train calling Midland at 11.55pm and around 10 parcels trains, among them the 11.58pm St. Pancras-Bradford, 8.15pm Bristol-Leeds, and the 10.55pm Carlisle-Sheffield. GC parcels trains included the 8.45pm Marylebone-Liverpool/Manchester Victoria and Preston, the 8.50pm Marylebone-York and 11.15pm Oldham Clegg Street-Marylebone.

The 1960s were a time of dramatic change and especially so for Sheffield's passenger services. As the decline of the GC gathered pace, the LM Region withdrew all through daytime trains between Marylebone and Sheffield from 4th January 1960. In their place were Nottingham-Marylebone semi-fasts and just one remaining overnight train each way between Marylebone and Sheffield - the Liverpool newspaper trains with limited passenger accommodation. The South Yorkshireman was replaced by a Halifax-St. Pancras service still serving Huddersfield which meant a reversal there. In summer 1961 this was the 8.45am from Halifax due into Midland station at 10.23 when two of its three coaches were attached to the 8.50am Bradford Forster Square-St. Pancras. The reverse procedure was followed with the return journey, the 5.5pm from St. Pancras which arrived at 8.28. The train was worked from Halifax by a Low Moor engine(Black Five No. 44990 on 19th August) which then worked the 12.51pm to Chinley, and back with the 3.48pm Stockport Tiviot Dale(3.56pm Manchester on Saturdays)-Sheffield before returning to Halifax.

By summer 1961 the midweek GC main line local service south of Sheffield stood at 11 Up trains(from Sheffield) and seven Down trains, all but one via Chesterfield. They ran variously between

The local service between Sheffield Victoria and Nottingham. D11/1 4-4-0 No. 62660 *Butler Henderson* leaves Renishaw Central at 4.47pm on 12th September 1959 with the 4.20pm Saturdays Only from Sheffield. *Neville Stead*

Sheffield, Chesterfield, Nottingham and Leicester with two of the Up trains from Manchester and one Down train to Manchester.

The Bournemouth, Swindon and overnight Liverpool trains were the only midweek expresses using the main line. On Friday nights and Saturdays an extra 15 main line trains ran, all seasonal. They included the 10am Bradford Exchange-Poole and 10.25 return, Newcastle and York-Swansea trains, a Manchester Piccadilly-Hastings each way, a Sheffield-Portsmouth Harbour each way, and a Chesterfield Central-Blackpool each way. BR stressed there was no intention to close the GC but that its future lay as a cross-country route via Banbury with freight predominating. Yet for winter 1960/61 the Newcastle-Bournemouth was reduced to a York-Banbury DMU!

Major remodelling completed at Barnsley over Easter 1960 enabled the through Sheffield-Barnsley-Leeds diesel service we know today. Previously, trains could go no further than Barnsley Court House. Another improvement in 1960 was a mainly hourly interval timetable on the electric service with trains leaving Sheffield at xx.45 and Manchester at xx.10.

The 1960s are always painfully associated with the ruthless line and station closures presided over by the then BR chairman Dr Richard Beeching. In fact, Beeching had little impact on Sheffield in terms of closures as the changes that took place during his tenure were happening anyway.

Pre-Beeching cuts included the Hull-Liverpool Central trains being cut back to run only between Victoria and Liverpool from the start of the winter 1962 timetable. The Sheffield Victoria-Chesterfield/Nottingham stopping service was axed in March 1963 upon closure of Chesterfield Central, Killamarsh Central and other intermediate stations - another nail in the coffin of the GC.

The most significant 1960s change within Sheffield affecting passenger services was remodelling and upgrading of the Nunnery curve so that it provided a direct route between Midland station and the GC lines to Retford and Doncaster. Along with a new

junction at Aldwarke(Rotherham) it enabled virtually all passenger services except the Manchester electrics to be concentrated on Midland station and on 4th October 1965 the King's Cross Pullmans were transferred there along with Doncaster, Hull, Cleethorpes, Retford and Lincoln services. Apart from the Manchester electrics, the only passenger services now using Victoria were the overnight Marylebone-Liverpool, the York-Bournemouth and York-Swindon trains, and the Harwich boat trains, now diesel-hauled throughout. That same year, Beeching unveiled a new plan for pruning the network even further and this time Sheffield would be affected. Passenger routes listed for development by 1984 were Sheffield-King's Cross, North East-South West, and Sheffield-Euston via Leicester and Rugby - no St. Pancras trains. "Beeching 2" was not implemented.

The following year brought more changes marking the final stage in the LM's run-down of the GC and development of the Midland. From 18th April 1966 the Midland main line timetable was completely re-cast to give hourly regular interval services between Sheffield and St. Pancras, trains alternately running via Derby and Nottingham. Leeds/Bradford trains and the remaining Anglo-Scottish trains were integrated into the Nottingham timetable. Then, from 5th September the York-Bournemouth and Swindon trains were switched to the Midland route and the entire GC main line from Beighton to Nottingham Arkwright Street closed to passenger traffic. It also meant withdrawal of the last timetabled passenger services over the GC line from Woodburn Junction to Aldwarke Junction and closure of Rotherham Central station. Victoria was left only with its increasingly isolated Manchester electrics and the boat trains.

By the late 1960s, The Master Cutler was running from King's Cross to Sheffield Midland in 2 hours 33 min. and from Midland to Kings Cross in 2 hr 35 min. Regardless of this, the King's Cross Pullmans were themselves withdrawn in October 1968 and the Master Cutler name bestowed on the 07.15 to St. Pancras and

Midland main line in the 1960s. BR/Sulzer "Peak" Type 4 No. D157 wheels the Up Thames-Cyde past Dore & Totley. *Tom Greaves*

17.55 return, but this was almost 10 minutes slower and it was no longer a Pullman but an "Executive" service. By May 1973 however, it was achieving the fastest time yet, two and half hours each way(the return by then 18.05 from London) calling only at Chesterfield and Leicester.

Victoria station, by now proposed for closure, took a further hit in 1969 when the boat trains were transferred to Midland, running via the Hope Valley and Nottingham. The Midland was not immune and that year also saw withdrawal of The Waverley as a general run-down of Midland line London-Scotland services got under way. The Glasgow sleeper services were rerouted to Euston from May 1969 but still called at Sheffield. By 1973 they were running between Glasgow and Nottingham only and the city would soon lose its Glasgow sleepers altogether. The Thames-Clyde lost its name in 1975 and in 1977 all St. Pancras-Glasgow services were withdrawn and replaced by Nottingham-Glasgow trains. By 1978 the West Yorkshire-St. Pancras service had dwindled to just one train from Leeds in the morning and one from London in the evening.

BR had been questioning the need for so many routes across the Pennines and the direct Midland route from Derby to Manchester had closed between Matlock and Buxton in 1967, its St. Pancras-Manchester expresses rerouted via the Dore South-West curve and the Hope Valley. By 1973 these were down to just two trains each way and by 1978 were running only on Sundays when they took up to six hours to complete the London-Manchester journey.

The future of the electrified line over Woodhead was not in doubt, but it was designated a trunk freight route and its passenger trains did not fit with BR's plans for concentrating all Sheffield services on Midland station. The electrically-hauled trains could not be rerouted to Midland as reversal at Nunnery would be impracticable, while mixing express passenger trains with heavy trunk freight was potentially disruptive. Consequently, the

Manchester-Sheffield Victoria service, electrified for less than 16 years, was withdrawn from 5th January 1970 and Victoria station closed. An almost like-for-like service but operated by class 1 DMUs running non-stop or stopping only at New Mills, was introduced on the Hope Valley where by 1969 the Sheffield service had comprised just a few stopping trains to Chinley or New Mills. The working timetable from 1st May 1972 shows, in addition to the New Mills all stations service, 14 class 1 DMUs departing Manchester Piccadilly at, as near as possible, xx.45 each hour(one continuing to Cleethorpes) and 15 from Sheffield at basically xx.15 past although the discipline could not be as closely maintained owing to two trains originating from Cleethorpes. The journey time was about an hour. Besides these were the Harwich boat trains(the Manchester departure integrated into the regular pattern at 14.40.) The last train of the day from Sheffield at 23.25 was loco hauled, as was the 01.50 Manchester Piccadilly-Cleethorpes news. A Penistone-Sheffield service was maintained by extending Huddersfield-Penistone DMUs to Sheffield Midland with a reversal at Nunnery. Diesel passenger trains would still be diverted over Woodhead during engineering work or other blockages.

The summer 1973 timetable shows the Manchester service increased to 18 fast trains from Sheffield and 14 into Sheffield including the boat trains. Of these, four originated from Hull, one from Scarborough via Hull, and two from Cleethorpes. In the opposite direction three continued to Hull and one to Cleethorpes. At this time, the Cleethorpes trains still went via Retford.

From the later 1970s Sheffield's leaders were demanding improvements to the St. Pancras service, especially once they saw how InterCity 125 High Speed Trains were decimating journey times on the East Coast main line through Doncaster while Sheffield still relied mainly on 90mph Type 4 "Peaks", Mk2 stock and in some cases a reversal at Nottingham. BR's view was that the Midland line had too many curves for the HSTs to achieve their full speed potential and thus, commercially, they were better deployed elsewhere. The Midland, said BR, should await electrification and the tilting Advanced Passenger Train. Electrification north of Bedford, however, wasn't even on the drawing board. Sheffield did get HSTs but on the increasingly important North East-South West route; from 5th October 1981 when they replaced loco-haulage on the 07.00 Bristol-Leeds, 08.20 Plymouth-Leeds, 14.37 Leeds-Plymouth and 16.38 Leeds-Bristol. A full HST timetable was implemented in May 1982 with 14 sets making big cuts in journey times. Then the economic recession of the early 1980s forced BR to review the use of its HST fleet and in October 1982 it transferred six sets to work eight Midland main line services each way, including the Master Cutler - not that they were able to do 125mph over much of it. Among routes to lose some of their HSTs was the North East-South West which consequently retained some loco-haulage into the 21st century.

During the 1980s, BR's passenger services came under the control of a new business sector management regime, the London and North East-South West services under InterCity and local services, including those to such places as Hull, Cleethorpes and East Anglia under Provincial Services, later renamed Regional Railways. InterCity immediately undertook a review of the St. Pancras service which included consideration to rerouting it via Retford and King's Cross. Instead, it improved standards on the St. Pancras route - including a facelift for Midland station. From 11th May 1987 the Master Cutler was returned to Pullman status. North East-South West was rebranded InterCity CrossCountry.

In the 1970s the metropolitan councils were made responsible for financially supporting and co-ordinating public transport in their areas and Sheffield came under the South Yorkshire County Council whose transport policy was administered by the South Yorkshire Passenger Transport Executive. The SYPTE's political masters initially seemed to be pro-bus, subsidising the country's cheapest bus fares and appearing to pay scant regard to rail. However, in 1977 the PTE began funding the Barnsley service, safeguarding its future. From January 1983 PTE support saw the Doncaster service improved to half hourly for much of the day. A Class 114 "Derby Works" DMU was repainted in SYPTE coffee and cream colours but unlike others, SYPTE stopped short of having new units of the 1980s repainted in its own livery as none ran exclusively in South Yorkshire. In 1986 the county council was abolished and a new passenger transport authority assumed its role. With it came new branding and blue/yellow colours for literature and station signs as well as station improvements, increased support for local services, and new and reopened stations such as Swinton and Rotherham Central.

A complete revision of Trans-Pennine services from 14th May 1979 brought a strengthening of the Hope Valley fast service. Class 124 Trans-Pennine units displaced from the route via Leeds were transferred to the route via Sheffield along with Class 123 Inter-City sets imported from the Western Region where they were previously in store. The 123s needed extensive restoration at Swindon Works and Lincoln depot to make them fit for public use. The five Hull-Manchester Piccadilly(six on Saturdays) through trains and three the other way were increased to 13 and 10 respectively, while the Cleethorpes service, which had faded to just one train each way, was increased to three from Manchester but remained at one from Cleethorpes plus one from Doncaster. It wasn't long before ordinary DMUs were having to deputise for the Inter-City sets and in May 1984 BR replaced them with loco-hauled trains, mainly using Class 31s.

A Western Region Inter-City set leads a DMU formation working a Birmingham service past Dore & Totley in the early 1960s. Just under twenty years later these units, as Class 123, would be back in greater numbers, based at Hull and working services from Manchester and Humberside. *Tom Greaves*

Throughout the 1980s Sheffield's Manchester service was in a constant state of flux, being revised year on year. By 1984 the fast service had changed to four trains from Hull and five from Manchester, but with three each way between Manchester and Cleethorpes, five Sheffield-Manchester and two Manchester-Sheffield plus one going on to York, a Nottingham-Glasgow/Edinburgh and Nottingham-Barrow each way, and the Harwich-Glasgow/Edinburgh boat train each way - a Class 47-hauled InterCity service now named The European. In 1986 a second boat train was inaugurated between Blackpool and Harwich.

The Glasgow, Barrow and Blackpool trains went via Manchester Victoria, giving Sheffield a direct link with the north side of Manchester. The following year The European was rerouted via London, the Sheffield service reverting to a Manchester-Harwich train, now called The Rhinelander. Meanwhile, the Blackpool boat train had been named The North West Dane. The Manchester-Hull/Cleethorpes trains had largely given way to a Liverpool-Sheffield service. Upon the opening of a new curve at Hazel Grove in 1986 class 1 trains were rerouted via Stockport giving Sheffield its first direct link with that town for many years.

A new stretch of line in Salford and the introduction of Class 156 Super Sprinter multiple units changed everything on the Hope Valley in May 1988. The service now consisted of two-hourly Blackpool-Cambridge or Ipswich Sprinters incorporating the Blackpool-Harwich boat train, now named The Loreley. Mixed with these were two-hourly Sheffield-Liverpool Sprinters and a single Liverpool-Norwich each way while the stopping service, now operated mostly by the much-troubled Pacer railbuses, was running throughout between Sheffield and Manchester. The new service pattern brought a 40 per cent increase in passengers after only a year and as a result was intensified to hourly Liverpool-East Anglia trains, the two-hourly Blackpool-East Anglia plus a 450-seat Nottingham-Blackpool loco-hauled train. In the early 1990s the 156s were replaced by the 90mph Class 158 sets still used in 2012. In 1994 Regional Railways supported by Derbyshire County Council and the Peak National Park began a more frequent Sunday stopping service in the Hope Valley in a bid to cut road traffic. It was branded The Hope Valley Explorer and brought back first generation Metro-Cammell DMUs - including one set restored to BR green livery - because they could accommodate rucksacks, bikes and push-chairs which the Pacers could not. They remained in use on the line into the 21st century when they were among the country's very last first generation DMU workings.

In January 1981 a revived weekday Sheffield-Chesterfield stopping service of six trains each way was introduced along with the reopening of Dronfield station under a joint initiative by BR and Derbyshire County Council.

By that time, the only passenger train using the Dore South-West curve was the 14.25 summer Saturday Blackpool-Leicester DMU. It was withdrawn at the end of the 1981 summer service and the curve became freight only - but for the temporary return of Manchester-St. Pancras HSTs in 2003/4 making up for a reduced Manchester-Euston service during the West Coast main line upgrading.

In the late 1970s Penistone's remaining passenger service came under threat, partly due to political brinkmanship, when it faced a succession of closure proposals. Upon confirming total closure of the Woodhead line between Penistone and Hadfield, BR proposed withdrawal of the Sheffield-Denby Dale portion of the Huddersfield service since neither South or West Yorkshire PTE

was prepared to fund it. The debate ran and ran until during a public hearing into a second closure proposal in March 1983, South Yorkshire dramatically announced that it would fund an experimental service via Barnsley for 12 months so long as BR could have it running by May. They succeeded and from the 16th Sheffield-Huddersfield trains were rerouted via Barnsley leading to a 42 per cent increase in passengers. The Nunnery Junction-Deepcar section was closed to passengers and the Deepcar-Barnsley Junction section completely, leaving Penistone as just a halt on a Barnsley-Huddersfield branch line.

In 1982 the Nottingham-Glasgow trains were rerouted via Manchester and the Hope Valley and, to avoid reversal at Midland station, via the Nunnery curve, Beighton and the Old Road. This ended Sheffield's 110 year-old Scottish service over the Midland route and reduced even further the number of trains between Sheffield and Leeds. A reasonable Sheffield-Leeds service was restored in 1986 with the start of five weekday Nottingham-Leeds trains each way. Two years later, an hourly stopping service via Rotherham Central and Moorthorpe was added.

A significant addition to Sheffield's passenger network in the 1990s was the Transport Authority's Meadowhall Interchange. A far cry from the old Wincobank station on the same site, it has platforms on both the Rotherham and Barnsley lines as well as a tram terminus and bus station, all linked to a vast retail complex.

Upon privatisation of BR in the 1990s, the St. Pancras service was taken over by Midland Main Line, CrossCountry by Virgin, North West-East Anglia by Central Trains, the Hope Valley stopping service by North West Trains, and local services within Yorkshire by Northern Spirit. The operators have all changed since.

In 2013 the Sheffield-St. Pancras journey - operated mostly by 125mph Class 222 Meridian DMUs - was boldly advertised as 2 hours 7 min. by the fastest of two trains every hour while some Down trains do it in 2 hours 5 min. The 07.27 to St. Pancras and 16.55 return still carry the Master Cutler name - some things are just too sacred to meddle with. In 2008 passengers and staff were asked to suggest names for two more trains and so the 06.47 from Sheffield is named The Sheffield Continental, and the 07.41 and 17.55 return The South Yorkshireman. The Master Cutler is no longer a Pullman but these Up morning services are referred to by the operator East Midland Trains as "Breakfast Trains," recalling the old 7.30am "Breakfast Car Special" from Victoria. A limited Leeds-St. Pancras service operates, mainly to get the route's HSTs to and from Neville Hill depot where they are maintained.

CrossCountry - operated since the early 21st century by 125mph Voyager Class 220 and 221 DMUs plus a handful of HSTs - has direct trains between Sheffield and places as far apart as Aberdeen, Penzance and Southampton - but not to Bournemouth at the time of writing, while trains run twice an hour hour to Birmingham. Two fast trains an hour run over the Hope Valley, one Norwich-Liverpool and one Cleethorpes-Manchester Airport. Sheffield-Barnsley-Leeds trains include Leeds, Sheffield and Nottingham expresses. As well as stopping trains via Rotherham Central, the Doncaster route sees CrossCountry and Manchester Airport-Cleethorpes expresses, and hourly Sheffield-Bridlington Northern Rail services via Meadowhall and Swinton. The GC line to Retford is served by just one Lincoln train an hour while the York stopping service consists of just two trains each way a day at times when they are not much good to anyone.

Freight

Such was the volume of freight generated by the heavy industry in and around Sheffield that in the 1950s/60s, the Sheffield Division was among BR's biggest revenue earners. In the mid-1960s the amount of originating freight was over 24 million tons a year, much of it from the 150 private sidings that served the countless steel works, forges, heavy engineering works, collieries, coke ovens and other concerns. That in turn meant an especially high number of trip workings between these sidings, the various sorting yards and goods depots in addition to all the freight trains passing into and out of the area.

A booklet produced by BR in 1965 to mark the opening of Tinsley marshalling yard described the organisation of freight operations around Sheffield when the Midland and GC lines still worked in isolation of each other: "In the middle 1950s the network of railways and depots remained much as it was at the turn of the century, despite the growth of competition in the interim, and major changes in the nature and pattern of the demand upon the railway for its services.

"The former LNER...had its main goods depot for small consignments at Bridgehouses, a coal depot at Harvest Lane, fruit and perishables at Blast Lane and wagon load traffic at Park Sidings, Attercliffe and West Tinsley....and a main marshalling yard at Bernard Road, with other yards at Broughton Lane, Ickles and Rotherham Road.

"The former LMSR...had an even greater multiplicity of depots and yards. These included depots for small consignments and wagon load traffic at Wicker and Queens Road, coal depots at Heeley and Nunnery, market traffic at Wharf Street, and wagon loads at Heeley, Pond Street, Brightside Wharf and Upwell Street Wharf....main marshalling yards at Masborough and Woodhouse Mill, with other yards at Grimesthorpe Engine Shed Sidings,

Wincobank, Roundwood, and Cardigan Sidings." Some locations referred to were in Rotherham.

"Facilities - passenger, freight handling, motive power - remained, in number, far beyond the real need in the new circumstances. The goods depots were out of date, cramped, lacking in mechanical aids and expensive to run; the marshalling yards were small and badly laid out; and the need to transfer so much traffic between the yards and depots was excessive, costly and conducive to transit delays."

Nationally, traffic had begun its inexorable decline in the late 1950s, yet just two years before the opening of Tinsley yard, goods trains were running constantly along the Sheffield area railways like the blood pumping through a giant's veins. So many were there that to describe them is a near impossible task.

The May-September 1963 working timetable reveals a staggering 800-plus freights per 24 hours each working day within an area bounded by Wincobank, Dunford Bridge, Dore & Totley, Killamarsh, Woodhouse and Treeton. Of these more than 240 were movements by local trips. These totals do not include the many light engines, trains which ran only on one or two days a week, or those which reached only the perifery of Sheffield, such as the Dore South-West or the Killamarsh-Waleswood curves. The main interchange points between the Midland and GC systems were via Woodhouse-Beighton, and Blackburn Valley-Meadow Hall where a reversal was necessary. An awkward manoeuvre involving reversal at Sheffield Midland or Nunnery Main Line Junction was sometimes used to reach Wharf Street and Nunnery yards.

On the GC lines, most of the 90-plus trains heading beyond Dunford Bridge per 24 hours were bound for Mottram yards at this time with those travelling east originating mainly from Dewsnap Sidings(Guide Bridge.) In the east, those that went via Sheffield were mainly to/from Staveley Central, Annesley, Warsop Junction or Mansfield Concentration Sidings, or Barrow Hill and

York WD 2-8-0 No. 90623 blasts away from Beighton on the GC main line with a southbound class 8 tank train at 11.10am on Saturday 24th November 1962. The Midland Old Road can be seen in the left distance. *Robert Anderson*

Seymour Junction on the Old Road as well as Sheffield's Bernard Road yard. Trains to/from such places as Frodingham, Doncaster, Hull, York and Cudworth travelled mainly via Wath. The vast majority going west were class 8 Through Freights consisting of unbraked loose-coupled wagons, mostly carrying coal while more of the empties eastbound ran class 7. Of highest priority were 3M39 5.13pm Grimsby-Ashton Moss and 4M40 7.45pm Hull-Manchester Park Sidings fish trains, the latter travelling via Wath. Another priority service was 4M12 the 9.51pm Grimsby Docks-Mottram Assured Arrival. Other fitted or partially fitted express freights of class 4 and 5 ran from Bridgehouses, Whitemoor, Leicester, New England, Ollerton Colliery Junction, Seymour Junction, Annesley, Lincoln, Immingham and Thames Haven to such places as Guide Bridge, Beswick, Ducie Street, Ordsall Lane, Ashburys, Northwich, Widnes, Glazebrook and Stretford as well as Mottram, some of them with assured arrival times. In the return, similar express freights ran mostly from Dewsnap, but also from Trafford Park, Ancoats, Huskisson, Ardwick and Northwich to Whitemoor, New England, Grimsby, Bernard Road, Bridgehouses, Mansfield Concentration Sidings, Seymour Junction, Immingham, Thames Haven, Hull, York and Woodford Halse. Paths were available on Tuesdays, Thursdays and Fridays for hauling locomotives to Darnall following repairs at Gorton Works and taking locos back again, likewise Mexborough(via Wath) on Mondays and Wednesdays.

Various local workings shuffled up and down east of Dunford Bridge, such as those between Bernard Road and Deepcar with traffic for Stocksbridge steel works and General Refractories, and specified electric haulage. Another was the 6.15am Bernard Road-Wadsley Bridge, also specified for an electric loco and an Assured Arrival service despite being class 8. Specified for diesel haulage was the 1.10pm Barnsley Junction-Hazelhead class 8 and 3.10pm return which also conveyed parcels for Hazelhead station and

shunted at Bullhouse. Petrol tanks came to Barnsley Junction on the 11.25pm from Stanlow and were tripped via Barnsley to and from a terminal at Ecclesfield West.

The GC main line east and south of Sheffield carried over 60 booked Up trains and around 55 in the Down direction, class 7 and 8s predominating during the daytime. Of the total, more than 20 each way took the Killamarsh-Langwith Junction LD&EC line, mainly the Mansfield and Warsop trains but also some express freights such as the Whitemoors travelling via Lincoln. Another ten each way interchanging with the Midland via Beighton Junction ran between Barrow Hill, Seymour Junction or Toton and Wath, Bernard Road, Broughton Lane, Ickles and Rotherham Road along with those crossing the Pennines. A handful of trains between Seymour Junction and Worksop or Grimsby reversed at Woodhouse. Around ten top priority express freights coming this way included the class 4 3.32am Woodford-Hull, 2.23pm Woodford-Tees, 4.40 and 6.35pm Woodford-York, 6.45pm Whitemoor-Stretford, 8.50pm Whitemoor-Manchester Ducie Street, 1.50am Whitemoor-Mottram, 6.10pm Burton-York, 12.45pm Barry Docks-Bradford Adolphus Street which ran when required, the 1.30am Hull-Annesley, 3.10am and 9.40pm Dringhouses-Woodford, 3.55am York-Banbury, 12.5am Tees-Cardiff and 2.20am Tees-Bristol.

Class 5 trains(continuous brake operating on not less than half the wagons) included the 9.15pm Leicester-Bernard Road, 1.30am Woodford-Bridgehouses, 5.53pm Woodford-Ardsley, 8.20pm Annesley-Wadsley Bridge, 12.20am Bernard Road-Annesley, 9.45pm Dewsnap-Whitemoor, 6.55am Bernard Road-Colwick and 8.5pm Ardwick-Annesley. Most trains to and from north of Sheffield continued via Attercliffe and Rotherham Central but a few, such as the 7.35am Woodford-York, travelled via Langwith Junction to reach the Old Road and the Midland route.

Relatively short-haul class 8 trains to and from such places as

Class EM1 No. 26031 heads an eastbound partially-fitted class 6 express goods through Dunford Bridge station in the 1960s. The remains of the original, pre-electrification station are on the right. *Tom Greaves*

Wath, Doncaster, Mexborough, Cudworth, Orgreaves, Worksop, Deepcar, Frodingham, Staveley, Annesley and Renishaw, predominated along the route from Woodburn and Darnall to Rotherham Central which saw around 35 booked freights in the Up direction(towards Rotherham) per 24 hours and around 50 in the Down. About a third were trip workings between various local sidings and Broughton Lane and Ickles yards. Longer distance trains consisted of those to and from the GC main lines already referred to plus the 10.42pm Bernard Road-York class 5(11.15 on Saturdays,) 6.50am York-Bernard Road class 8 and the 10.35pm Hull-Bernard Road class 6. Also class 5 was the 11.20pm Greasborough Road(Rotherham)-High Dyke iron ore empties.

The Tinsley-Meadow Hall section of the old GC Barnsley line was by then used mostly for short trips between Ickles or Broughton Lane and the various works at Meadow Hall, Grange Lane or Ecclesfield East plus interchanges with the Midland lines via Blackburn Valley Junction. Only one train each way ran throughout between Ickles and Wath.

The Old Road was then - and still is - a major freight artery. The summer 1963 working timetable showed around 80 booked freights each way along the stretch between Killamarsh West and Treeton besides those transferring to and from the GC via Beighton Junction. Fifteen on the Down and a dozen on the Up were local trips, mainly between Woodhouse Mill Sidings and the various local yards on the Midland side of Sheffield such as Wincobank, Roundwood, Wicker, Firth's Sidings and Upwell Street, as well as Treeton Colliery. Again, the vast majority of trains were class 8 but there were plenty of long-distance express freights of the highest priority, most of them at night. Top of the list was 3S60 the 7.23pm Hendon-Glasgow Gushetfaulds and 3M29 the 7.50pm Gushetfaulds-Hendon container trains - the

famous "Condor" - forerunner of today's Freightliner services and, originally hauled by the ill-starred Metrovick Co-Bo diesels. Train 3S60 was booked past Beighton Junction at 10.56pm and 3M29 at 2.9am. Among no less than 24 class 4 fully fitted trains on the Up and 15 on the Down were the 12.30am Greenhill-Wilshamstead, 3.25am Carlisle-Stoke Gifford, 5.20am and 12.40pm Carlisle and 6.18pm Glasgow-Washwood Heath, 5.45pm Hurlford-Brent, 5.45pm Glasgow, 6.45pm Bradford, 8.20pm Stourton and 5.35pm Carlisle-St. Pancras, 12.20am Willesden-Carlisle, 7.35am Woodford-York, 4.25pm Leicester-Carlisle, 2pm Somers Town-Masborough, 2.55pm Bristol-Dringhouses, 6.10pm Burton-York, 4.55pm Water Orton-Carlisle, and 8.27pm Luton-Bonniebridge when required. The daytime class 4s included a succession of fully fitted iron ore trains from Wellingborough and Storefield to Normanby Park(Scunthorpe) or West Hartlepool as required, and often entrusted to Wellingborough's Crosti 9Fs. A notable class 4 was the 10.10pm St Pancras-Bridgehouses going via Woodhouse.

The route via Sheffield Midland between Dore and Wincobank is often stated as principally a passenger line but in 1963 it carried a mindboggling array of booked freights with over 90 on the Down and nearly 170 on the Up. Most were local trips and class 8s shuffling between the yards, depots and sidings in the heavily industrialized area between Grimesthorpe, Wincobank and Masborough. But plenty of freights passed through Midland station, mostly at night, including 20-plus class 4 - 6 expresses northbound and about a dozen southbound; only a minority were to and from the Hope Valley. The priority train was 3M15, the 9.15pm York-Birmingham fish calling Midland 11.28pm-midnight, along with 4M78 the 1.25am fish from Midland to Birmingham. Class 4s included the 4.45pm Water Orton-Glasgow, 8.2pm Burton-Carlisle, 4.48pm Bristol-Hunslet Lane, the 11.45pm

At the time of writing virtually all freight via Sheffield Midland is to and from the Hope Valley which can go no other way, but back in the 1960s it represented only a fraction of the traffic passing through. On Saturday 20th July 1963, Barrow Hill-based 8F 2-8-0 No. 48396 boosts the Hope Valley traffic level by taking the Chinley line at Dore & Totley with a special class 8 unfitted train.

John Beaumont/Robert Anderson archive

Carlisle-Leicester Assured Arrival, 9.10pm Stourton-Lawley Street, and the 6.15pm Garston-Masborough Sorting Sidings from the Hope Valley, running when required.

During this time the District Railway had no booked trains between Catcliffe and Tinsley Park Colliery Sidings. The odd trip between the two had to travel via Treeton and Masborough sorting sidings. Others ran from the Brightside end to serve the steel plants at Tinsley and Shepcote Lane.

In 1960 the Sheffield area rationalisation project was given the go-ahead. At its heart was the massive new Tinsley marshalling yard, situated on the District Railway and designed to replace the smaller yards. New curves connecting the District Railway to the GC line at Tinsley(north facing) and Broughton Lane(south facing,) and the Old Road at Treeton North(north facing) along with a new junction connecting the Midland and GC lines at Aldwarke(Rotherham) where they passed close to each other enabled freight trains to access the new yard from any direction, Midland or GC. The scheme included a new central freight terminal for Sheffield situated on the site of Grimesthorpe motive power depot and C&W shops which were to close.

In the space of five years the Sheffield freight network changed beyond recognition as goods facilities were progressively rationalised in the run-up towards final completion in 1965. Pond Street closed on 19th September 1960 - its site earmarked for Sheaf House, the new Divisional Manager's office block - and West Tinsley followed just two weeks later. Blast Lane closed on 6th November 1961, Brightside Wharf and Upwell Street Wharf on 1st April 1963, Queen's Road on 13th May and Park on 1st June. Wharf Street and Wicker closed on 12th July 1965 commensurate with the opening of the new freight terminal while Bridgehouses followed on 2nd October. Harvest Lane, Nunnery, Darnall, Attercliffe and Broughton Lane depots survived owing to the specialized traffic they handled.

Describing the new Sheffield freight terminal, the BR booklet stated: "The Sheffield freight terminal has been designed to cater for all forwarded and received small consignments in the entire Sheffield Division, including Sheffield, Barnsley, Rotherham and Chesterfield. Traffic for depots outside Sheffield, previously moved by rail to and from Sheffield, will be conveyed direct by road motor vehicles based on the new terminal. It also acts as a residual tranship depot for sundries traffic for which through wagons cannot be made, and deals with warehouse and wagon load traffic formerly accommodated at Bridgehouses, Wicker, Queens Road and Wharf Street."

The terminal comprised a 920ft long goods shed covering around 25,000 square yards, divided into two sections for received and forwarded sundries of up to 600 tons a day. These were still manhandled from the wagons onto trolleys which were then hauled in "trains" along a raised deck to berths at the delivery front for loading onto road vehicles. Alongside the sundries shed was a 960ft long warehouse with storage stacking up to 20ft high. The yard could accommodate 200 rail wagons and outside equipment included loading docks, mobile cranes and a 35 ton Goliath crane with standage for 56 wagons underneath. There was also a workshop for maintaining road vehicles and handling equipment.

Upon commissioning of Aldwarke Junction in March 1965, many heavy through freights previously using the GC main line to and from the south were rerouted to the Midland and the Old Road, avoiding the steep gradients to Woodburn Junction which peaked at 1 in 70, and eliminating the need for two banking engines. On 14th June all through mineral trains were diverted from the GC main line to the Midland. Tinsley Yard came on stream during 1965 and the various sorting yards were either closed or reduced to cover purely local needs, Broughton Lane being retained as a concentration point for private siding traffic. Tinsley was now the central hub to which all originating wagonload freight was tripped for marshalling into trainloads using state-of-the-art hump shunting systems, and vice-versa for incoming traffic.

The BR booklet describes thus the transition to Tinsley and the new freight routes radiating from it: "Since July this year, under Stage 1 of the plan for commissioning the yard, when traffic was absorbed from the ex-Midland yards, through loads have been

This BR publicity photo from 1965 shows the sundries dock inside the new Sheffield central freight depot.
In the late 1960s the warehouse part of the terminal was transferred to state-owned National Carriers Ltd.
It was destroyed in 1984 by a fire which sent huge clouds of toxic smoke and asbestos into the air over Sheffield. The site is now occupied by a Royal Mail sorting centre which is not rail-connected.

made up for Toton, Norton Junction, Washwood Heath, Healey Mills, Chaddesden, Leeds, Stanton Gate, Frodingham, Mottram, St. Pancras, Gowhole, Leicester, Brent and Port Talbot. Additional outlets to Hunslet, Nottingham, Carlisle, York and Glasgow have been provided by through freight services calling at Tinsley.

"With the commencement of the winter timetable, this October, traffic was absorbed from the former GC yards and through services provided to Lincoln, New England, Hull, Birkenhead, Liverpool Brunswick, Colwick, Doncaster, Whitemoor, King's Cross, Ferme Park and Worksop. It was expected at this stage the yard would be working near to the planned capacity of 4,000 wagons per day but, in the light of experience under actual working conditions, consideration will be given to transferring some of the remaining work from Masborough Sorting Sidings to Tinsley, and to the extent to which work can be absorbed from further afield."

These latter words tell their own story. As with all the big 1960s marshalling yards, the traffic for which Tinsley was designed was already in decline. Handling multitudes of individual and part wagon loads from a multiplicity of origins to a multiplicity of destinations was labour-intensive and loss-making for BR. Ever since the 19th century the railways had been obliged by law to accept all such traffic but that had changed and BR could now pursue its policy of concentrating on block trainloads between terminals and private sidings. In any case, general freight involving small loads and complex distribution had for years been shifting to the roads while remaining general traffic would move to Freightliner. Even so, the nature of Sheffield freight with 80 per cent of traffic being of local origin or destination and 70 per cent of that being to or from private sidings, often handling but a few wagons at a time, saw to it that wagonload traffic would continue for years to come. Furthermore, it was envisaged that plans to transfer most trans-Pennine freight to the Woodhead line would maintain a high traffic level.

The new train plan arrangements just mentioned, were an attempt to accommodate wagonload traffic in the most efficient and cost-effective manner possible. Under the 1968 Transport Act, the sundries part of the freight terminal was transferred to a new state-run haulage company called National Carriers Limited. NCL was very much road-orientated and from then on rail traffic declined steadily until the warehouse became a road haulage depot. The outdoor facilities continued to handle BR wagonload traffic.

The shift of cross-Pennine freight to the Woodhead line went ahead but in 1971 the massive new power station at Fiddlers Ferry, near Warrington, came on stream and from the outset it was fed with Yorkshire and East Midlands coal by a constant procession of air-braked 1000-ton merry-go-round trains routed via Woodhead. A look at the May 1972 working timetable illustrates the intensity of freight over the Woodhead line shortly after withdrawal of passenger trains and the start of Fiddlers Ferry - especially west of Penistone where traffic from Wath yards joined that from Sheffield. Every 24 hours, round the clock, from Tuesday to Friday (as on most lines, many freights did not run on Monday mornings) there were over 70 westbound freights and over 60 eastbound, less than 1963 but often with bigger loads. Of these only 14 westbound and 13 eastbound were Mandatory which ran come-what-may. The rest were conditional on traffic but they did include around two dozen class 6 Fiddlers Ferry MGRs each way consisting of 30-32 high capacity hopper wagons. Most of the remainder were class 8, including coal trains formed of traditional mineral wagons to Garston Dock. Just 12 booked trains originated at Tinsley Yard, and seven terminated there. In addition were a small number of company block trains, including the 04.00 Widnes-Broughton Lane train of BOC(British Oxygen) tanks on Wednesdays, Thursdays and Fridays and its 15.20 return, the Humber Oil Refinery-Holyhead petroleum coke train(and return empties,) a Hull-Garston Freightliner each way and various oil trains. The latter included 6E37 which ran overnight from Ellesmere Port to Pontefract Baghill, Warsop, Tuxford or Gainsborough Lea Road as

A merry-go-round coal train to Fiddlers Ferry snakes beneath a mass of catenary structures behind EM1 Bo-Bos 76037 and 76038 as it approaches Huddersfield Junction, Penistone, on a raw Friday 3rd April 1981. *Stephen Chapman*

required. A Leeds-Holyhead Freightliner serving Sheffield was suspended at the time. Three others of note were the 01.12 Manchester Piccadilly-Cleethorpes news, 22.10 Manchester Mayfield-Liverpool Street parcels and the 13.46 Nunnery-Longsight empty stock. At the western end, the class 8 freights were mainly to or from Ashburys, Dewsnap or Godley Junction where they were made up or split for individual wagon destinations all over Cheshire and Lancashire. At the eastern end, most were from or to Wath, Rotherwood or Tinsley, although some of those were also to and from further afield. Often, the same MGR working would start from Wath or Rotherwood as required. Yorkshire coal mainly came via Wath and Nottinghamshire coal via Rotherwood. With so many class 8 trains one can see how difficult it would have been mixing these with class 1 passenger trains. The freights would spend so much time "inside" at points along the way that a backlog would surely build up with heavy delays as a result.

The 1972 working timetables also reveal the pattern of freight working then pertaining around Sheffield. And given today's circumstances it is hard to imagine just how much there still was in post-steam and Beeching times. Many trains running direct between the North, Midlands and South ran via the Old Road and missed Sheffield or Tinsley while others were routed via the yard for inspection and to pick-up and detach wagons. Although reduced since 1965, trains went to and came from other big marshalling yards at Toton, Bescot, Healey Mills, Tees and Carlisle and others to and from Glasgow, Workington, Teesport, Hull, York, Leeds, Doncaster, Scunthorpe, Worksop, Leicester, Nottingham and Warrington. Many were still class 8. One train of slightly higher status was the 21.55 merchandise from St. Pancras Goods, a class 6 with continuous braking on at least 20 per cent of the wagons, as was the 02.10 to Teesport. About two thirds of the booked trains starting and originating at Tinsley were classed as conditional and may or may not run or may be routed elsewhere, such as Rotherwood.

Rotherwood Sidings, where diesel and electric traction were exchanged for those trains crossing the Pennines, saw around 60 trains come and go each 24 hours Tuesday-Friday. Of these 17 were "Fiddlers" MGRs. The remainder were mainly class 8. Through trains were en- route Wallerscote and Northwich(both ICI)-Whitemoor; Toton-Edge Hill, Garston, Ashburys and Glazebrook; Whitemoor-Ashburys; Mansfield Concentration Sidings-Garston and Ardwick; and Immingham-Runcorn. Among several diesel-hauled trains passing by were a couple of Worksop-Tinsley trips as well as the 18.58 Norwood-Broughton Lane on Mondays and Fridays and 18.30 Fletton-Broughton Lane on Wednesdays. On Thursdays a train ran from Whitwell, near Worksop, to Oughty Bridge, the engine and brake van returning to Worksop around mid-day.

Much of the traffic still using the Woodburn Junction-Rotherham line consisted of freights to and from Tinsley Yard. Apart from the Broughton Lane trains already mentioned, others not doing so were - as at the time of writing - those between the steel works at Aldwarke and Stocksbridge. They included the 02.15 Teesport-Deepcar and 07.28 Deepcar-Teesport class 6 which also conveyed traffic for Tinsley Park works as required and changed crews at Shepcote Lane; and the 14.10 Aldwarke-Warrington booked to take on an electric loco during a lengthy stand in a siding until 17.00 at Woodburn Junction. The Freightliner trains travelled via Tinsley Yard in order to access Sheffield terminal which was on the Old Road at the site of Rotherham Masborough sorting sidings.

The few freights passing through Midland station by the 1970s included overnight cement trains from Earles Sidings to Dewsbury and Middlesbrough, a return daytime Earles-Wath, and a couple of Tinsley-Earles and Peak Forest trips.

Engineers trains ran on certain days of the week between Crofton(Wakefield) and Beighton depot, along with a Narborough-Beighton ballast train. The oil terminal at Ecclesfield West on the ex-Midland Barnsley line was served by nightly trains from Stanlow(now via the Hope Valley) and Teesport, the latter running round at Brightside. It should not be overlooked that even in the 1970s, the booked trains mentioned were only part of the story. Local trips continued to ply their trade between the various plants, private sidings and depots.

Diesel meets electric at Rotherwood Sidings on Tuesday 19th August 1980. EM1 No. 76003 awaits departure with the 11.30 coal to Garston while Brush Type 2 No. 31279 passes by on a trip working towards Sheffield. *Stephen Chapman*

A particularly notable freight flow emerging in the 1970s - not least because of its name - is SMACC and SPACE. These are the two stainless steel plants at Tinsley Park(SMACC) and Shepcote Lane(SPACE,) each connected by private siding to Tinsley Yard. Steel cast at SMACC was taken by rail to Grimsby or Goole where it was shipped to Sweden or Germany for making into coil and then returned to SPACE for finishing and distribution. They came to generate around 5,000 tonnes of traffic a week.

Still grappling with the wagonload problem, BR wanted rid of the old short-wheelbase, unbraked or vacuum braked wagons which were slow, ill-suited to modern loading methods and prone to derailment. During the 1970s it introduced a new network air-braked wagonload trains running to passenger-style timetables at speeds up to 75mph. It was called Speedlink and with it came new long wheelbase freight vehicles and a new fleet of 3,250hp Class 56 locomotives - the first BR diesel locomotives built purely for heavy freight. Tinsley depot would have a substantial allocation. A new range of hopper wagons was also introduced for coal traffic which was not MGR. Even so, Tinsley was not to be a major point on the Speedlink network and continued dealing mainly with class 7 and 8 trains. It would only be served by Speedlink trains calling there while en-route between other yards, such as in May 1979 the 19.52 Hunslet-Dover, 21.27 Dringhouses-Eastleigh, 19.10 Margam-Hull and 17.15 Dover-Dringhouses.

With Speedlink well established by the early 1980s, BR sought to eliminate all remaining unfitted loose-coupled wagons. Especially targeted were the classic 16-ton mineral wagons and that led to a storm at which Sheffield was the centre. Across the country scrap merchants depended on these wagons for sending scrap to the furnaces of Sheffield and Rotherham. Now BR told them they must buy their own but most were small individual concerns lacking the necessary capital, and their only option was to switch up to 600,000 tonnes of traffic a year to road transport. By 1984 the argument was finally resolved through a leasing deal with the Standard Wagon Company of Heywood, Rochdale, and a £2.52 million government grant for 293 new 51-tonne air-braked box wagons, keeping a substantial amount of Sheffield's incoming freight on the rails - at least for the time being. But many other local freight customers were cut off and turned to the roads.

The 1980s began with a destructive economic recession, presided over by a government unsympathetic to "dirty" heavy industry with its trade unions. It saw the banking and financial services sector as the key to Britain's future prosperity. The recession brought a massive collapse in Sheffield's traditional industries. Works and forges went out of business one after the other as did the coking works that fed them and whole industrial areas became wastelands.

This almost total collapse of manufacturing along with the virtual elimination of coal mining wiped out most of Sheffield's originating freight traffic and with it numerous private industrial railways. By 1984 most local traffic consisted of steel and scrap, Sheffield Freight Terminal traffic - again mostly steel - and fruit for Parkway Market situated on a private siding behind Darnall depot. The throughput of wagons at Tinsley had plunged to 5,000 a week, and was halved by the 1984/85 miners' strike. The Woodhead line had also closed and its remaining freight diverted to other routes away from Sheffield.

Then, within 15 years of its inception, Speedlink was gone - shut down in 1991 by Railfreight Distribution, the BR business which then operated it - blaming massive losses. Switching their traffic

to Freightliner or less frequent trainloads were the only alternatives offered to wagonload customers. For many these were not practicable and at a stroke Sheffield wagonload customers surviving into the 1990s were cut off and forced to use road transport. Steel and scrap traffic were switched to a new Trainload Metals network operated by BR's Trainload Freight business and it was to this business which Tinsley yard became dedicated.

Sheffield Freight Terminal's main traffic by the late 1980s had been such commodities as outgoing bricks to Scotland and export machinery besides its staple diet of steel, served by a regular trip working from Tinsley and block trains as required. Local road cartage was provided by Exel Logistics, formerly NCL.

In 2012 the only private sidings still functioning in Sheffield were Stocksbridge steel works, Attercliffe goods yard - long since a metal recycling centre - and SMACC and SPACE which provide just about the only rail traffic in the small remnant of Tinsley Yard. A rail-served freight terminal has been built on the site giving some future hope. Sheffield Freight Terminal closed in 1990(the NCL portion being destroyed by fire in 1984) and most of Sheffield's railborn freight, mostly steel, is handled at Rotherham freight depot which occupies the site of the long-abandoned Freightliner terminal. What remains of the Woodhead line sees a single return trip each night between Aldwarke and Deepcar, a weekly train of export scrap in loaded bogie box wagons runs from Attercliffe to Liverpool Docks, and along with Outokumpu traffic(formerly SMACC and SPACE) that's about it for Sheffield's originating freight trains. Heavy freights still pass through the area mostly via the Old Road paying no heed to Sheffield and much reduced in number, or through Midland station en-route to and from the quarries and cement works of the Peak District. Almost all steel traffic is now centred on Rotherham.

All change

Anyone familiar with Sheffield's railway network, be they an enthusiast or railway staff, will be acutely aware of its painful decline since the start of the 1980s. If Tinsley Yard were its beating heart then Sheffield's railway would be dead but, like Dr. Who, it has two hearts and Midland station continues to be its strength. More than ever, it is a major hub for long distance and local passenger journeys but the freight infrastructure, once some of the busiest in the country, has faded almost to extinction.

Apart from the Manchester, Sheffield & Wath electrification, there were few dramatic changes to the Sheffield railway scene between 1903 and the 1960s yet the city was often at the leading edge of railway technology, from the first mass-produced steel rails to Britain's first all-electric main line. More would follow.

The electrification was first mooted in the 1920s to overcome the extreme and difficult operating conditions experienced with steam. The LNER began work in 1937 and by the time the second world war forced a halt, masts for the overhead wires were starting to appear and a prototype Class EM1 Bo-Bo electric loco was nearing completion. Construction of the new motive power depot at Darnall continued and it opened in 1943.

After the war, work resumed and prototype loco No. 6701(6000 from 1946) was sent for test running on the Netherlands Railways where they used the same 1500 volt dc system. While there it was christened *Tommy* by Dutch railwaymen in gratitude to the British soldiers who had liberated them from the Nazis. Following some design improvements, construction of another 57 EM1s began. A plan to use ex-North Eastern electric locos, redundant from the de-electrified Shildon-Newport line, as banking engines(Class EB1 - electric banker) was dropped in favour of EM1s. Seven Class EM2 Co-Co express passenger locomotives were built from 1954.

The most challenging of numerous civil engineering works required was the construction of an entirely new double track. Woodhead Tunnel to replace the two claustrophobic single bores. New exchange sidings complete with a 70ft turntable were laid out at Rotherwood, just west of Woodhouse to facilitate the exchange of steam and electric locomotives on freight trains. An electric locomotive servicing shed was built at Darnall. Although not in the original plan, colour light signalling was installed.

The first section, up the 1 in 40 Worsborough bank from Wath to Dunford Bridge began operating in February 1952 and Manchester to Woodhead in June 1954. The Woodhead Tunnel and Penistone-Woodburn sections had been completed by September 1954 and Britain's first electric inter-city passenger service was inaugurated on the 20th, following a fanfare opening ceremony at Woodhead on the 14th. At this point Sheffield could boast Britain's most advanced railway, not least with the cutting edge regenerative braking fitted to the locomotives that fed power back into the overheads as they descended steep gradients. It was almost the perfect railway and increased line capacity by 50 per cent. The final section from Woodburn to Rotherwood was commissioned in February 1955. Upon electrification, steam locomotives were banned from Woodhead Tunnel under their own power. Passenger trains to and from Manchester changed locomotives between electric and steam at Victoria, freights at Rotherwood and Wath. Steam could still run between Penistone and Sheffield, such trains as The South Yorkshireman remaining steam throughout.

The 1958 reorganisation already referred to saw everything east of Woodhead, including the Midland lines from Horns Bridge (Chesterfield) to Darfield, pass to the Eastern Region under the jurisdiction of the newly established Sheffield District Traffic Manager. North of Darfield they went to the North Eastern Region. Everything west of Dunford Bridge and south of Pilsley on the GC main line went to the London Midland. With two main lines to London, the LM as already related, began to run-down the GC. The Eastern found itself with three motive power depots in Sheffield(not to mention those elsewhere in the district,) two main line stations operating services to the East Midlands and London, two control offices in charge of its lines, and a plethora of competing goods yards and private sidings. Sorting this all out needed massive infrastructure work and so with BR facing mounting losses the ER planners rushed to their drawing boards. In 1960 the £11 million Sheffield rationalisation and modernisation scheme received Parliamentary powers. With improving efficiency of freight operations uppermost, Tinsley marshalling yard was at its heart but the concentration of all passenger services on Sheffield Midland was another benefit that would be reaped from the installation of the new lines referred to earlier. Excluding dieselisation, the scheme was expected to save £1.2 million a year

The only site available for the new yard was on the District Railway between Shepcote Lane and Catcliffe which, but for being mostly undeveloped with about half the land already in railway ownership, was hardly ideal. Standing in the way was land rising 60ft above track level, and over 3.75 million tons of sandstone and shale had to be excavated to level the site which in total covered 145 acres; a two-mile private road had to be built to carry the spoil to colliery tipping grounds at Orgreave. Even so, there was still a 1 in 100 rising gradient from Catcliffe Viaduct to the reception sidings. Land totalling 115 acres had to be bought from 12 different owners with matters further complicated by the need to provide a new site for a forge planned by Firth Vickers. The Sheffield & South Yorkshire Canal had to be diverted, bridged and a new lock built, and provision made for the proposed M1.

The cutting wall behind master & slave shunter No. D4500 at Tinsley Yard shortly after opening illustrates the scale of excavation required to level the site. *Tom Greaves*

When complete the vast complex comprised 11 reception roads each capable of taking 63-74 wagons, 53 main sorting sidings arranged in eight "balloons," 25 secondary sorting sidings mainly for local traffic in four "balloons," and a five-road express freight yard for through trains calling to attach and detach wagons. Wagons were sorted by means of two humps, one to feed each sorting yard. The speed of wagons descending the hump was regulated by the world's first complete application of the Dowty hydraulic retarder system. It used closely-spaced speed retarders/ boosters and speed sensors to predict the speed of wagons and adjust it accordingly, and was considered a major advance on earlier electronic methods.

Wagons were directed into appropriate sidings from two control towers, one for the main yard and one for the secondary yard. To push them over the humps, six 350hp diesel shunters were converted to three 700hp 0-6-0-0-6-0 "master & slave" units.

Accompanying the yard was the new diesel traction depot situated on a higher level at the south side. It would not only replace Darnall but would meet locomotive requirements far beyond Sheffield. Within the yard, a servicing depot was provided along with various other facilities including a breakdown crane shed and a cattle dock for attending to livestock in transit. Electrification was extended to the yard from Woodburn Junction. New signal boxes were built at Tinsley Park, Tinsley Yard, Shepcote Lane and Brightside Junction. The scheme included new wagon shops at Woodhouse Mill but the redundant Darnall MPD was used instead. The whole lot was formally opened by Dr Beeching on 29th October 1965 when Tinsley was declared Europe's most modern marshalling yard.

Most local stations had closed during the 1950s and there were some minor line closures. First during the BR era was the Spital Hill Tunnel branch, others were the Birley Colliery branch around 1950 and the Tinsley Park Colliery branch in 1958. Nunnery Colliery and its railway had also closed by then. The Meadow Hall-Blackburn Valley curve was severed and reduced to sidings by 1965 while the Wicker branch closed with Wicker goods depot in July 1965, surviving portions being absorbed into Firth Brown's works. The GC Barnsley line ceased to be a through route in March 1966 after which it went no further than Smithywood coking plant at Chapeltown. After 4th September 1966 the only part of the GC main line remaining immediately south of Sheffield were nine-miles from Beighton Station Junction to Arkwright Colliery at Duckmanton. The LD&EC had also ceased to be a through route to Langwith Junction, three miles from Beighton Junction being retained to serve Westthorpe Colliery at Spink Hill. The Waleswood curve had also gone by this time and the Killamarsh Branch to Kiveton Park Colliery would soon follow. The Hepworth Iron Company's branch had closed by 1969 and the Wincobank North-West curve was being worked as a siding.

High on BR's agenda in the 1970s was track rationalisation and signalling modernisation throughout South Yorkshire. Stage one included reduction to two running lines between Heeley and Dore & Totley and closure of the underpass line, its northern end being retained for use with a carriage washer. The new Sheffield power signal box was commissioned in January 1973, replacing Midland station's five mechanical boxes plus four others en-route to Millhouses. Over the rest of the decade PSB control and multiple aspect signalling were progressively extended across the whole area. In 1982 BR was awarded a £1.65 million European grant towards the £15 million Stage two, extending Sheffield control to freight lines around Rotherham and Mexborough by 1983. One exception up to the time of writing has been the GC line east of Nunnery which remains under the control of Woodburn Junction and Woodhouse Junction boxes.

During the 1970s the vexed question of over-capacity on the trans-Pennine routes reared its head again. The number of freight trains crossing the Pennines was declining, not just over Woodhead but also on the alternative routes due to a number of factors, not just loss of traffic but bigger trains meaning fewer trains. In 1979 BR announced its intention to close the Woodhead line altogether, citing not just declining traffic but that the infrastructure and locomotives were obsolete, non-standard and would soon need renewing while the estimated £44 million cost of a standard 25kv AC system could not be justified. BR also argued that changing from diesel loco to electric loco and back to diesel was inefficient and that rerouting traffic would only require 10 more diesels to replace 45 electrics. Strong opposition came from local authorities, the railway unions and other pressure groups who argued that the line would be needed in the future. The three alternatives: the Hope Valley, Calder Valley, the Diggle route, all had passenger services - the latter two serving sizeable towns with PTE funding - while the Woodhead line was freight only so taking all into consideration, the odds were stacked against it.

Thus, the Penistone-Hadfield section of Sheffield's first main line and the Woodhead Tunnel closed completely with effect from 20th July 1981. BR agreed to retain the track and overhead line structures for six months(in the event track remained until 1986) but the overhead wires were quickly recovered before they could be stolen. A railway still runs through Woodhead Tunnel at the time of writing - a 2ft gauge line laid through one of the old bores in 1969 to service high voltage National Grid cables. The Barnsley Junction-Nunnery section stayed open to for the Sheffield-Huddersfield service until that was rerouted via Barnsley in 1983 when the Barnsley Junction-Deepcar section closed completely. Nunnery-Deepcar has since been reduced to single track for the freight trains to Stocksbridge steel works that pass through the totally redeveloped Victoria station site. A loop was retained at Wadsley Bridge for football specials using the station there.

The relentless decline in heavy industry and manufacturing, not just in Sheffield but across the whole of Britain since the 1970s, has seen most steel works and heavy engineering plants in the Brightside, Grimesthorpe and Meadow Hall area disappear and those that remain are no longer directly served by rail. The big coking plants at Smithywood, Orgreave and Brookhouse have all closed, their attendant railways and associated industries with them. All the numerous private sidings and yards along the GC Woodburn Junction-Rotherham line have gone. Arkwright Colliery closed in the 1980s and the last local remnant of the GC's London main line with it. Spink Hill went about the same time and so this stretch of the LD&EC was abandoned, leaving just a short run-round at the Beighton Junction end. The last section of the GC Barnsley line closed in 1987 following the demise of Smithywood, this branch also subject to an unsuccessful preservation attempt. Nunnery carriage sidings were closed in 1986.

As for Tinsley Yard, it has been a sorry tale of decline towards oblivion. By 1984 the yard was being scaled down to a facility designed to handle just 400 wagons a day instead of the 5,000 it was originally designed for. Just 27 roads of the main sorting yard remained, plus the express freight yard for use as reception sidings and staging block loads. Sixteen roads of the main yard were used for storing condemned wagons en-route to local scrap yards and the secondary yard, reduced to dead-end roads, for holding passenger stock awaiting asbestos removal - it would be abandoned once that was cleared. The hump was out of use along with the Dowty retarders. The long-term future of the adjacent diesel maintenance depot was stated as secure.

The decline of Tinsley also signalled the end for the District Railway, the Brightside-Shepcote Lane section closing and the Tinsley-Treeton portion falling into disuse. In 2012 the rusting track through Catcliffe remained but with sections missing and overgrown. Only the express freight yard has ultimately survived to deal with such traffic as remains. In 2012 the Sheffield International Rail Freight Terminal occupied a large part of the site but the sidings were rusty and the 647,000sq ft warehouses appeared vacant. In December 2012 a large aggregates company was granted planning permission for a rail-served aggregates depot with roadstone and ready-mixed concrete plants there.

Tinsley depot survived the yard's decline and became Railfreight Distribution's principal diesel depot for England and Wales. RfD became the last part of BR to be privatised and thus Tinsley could claim the distinction of being the last diesel loco depot on BR. However, when RfD was sold to the private English, Welsh & Scottish Railway in 1997 its new owners declared Tinsley depot superfluous, and shut it down in 1998.

The 1990s saw development of the Supertram network and its construction had a further impact on the railway. This included singling of the Woodburn Junction-Tinsley section and use of the abandoned road as one of the two Supertram lines to Meadowhall Interchange(opened 1990) and the massive shopping centre selling imported goods where once huge engineering plants manufactured goods for sale to the world. Much of the Nunnery sidings site is now occupied by the Parkway main road, offices, and the Supertram depot. Despite all the decline, Sheffield will still be at the forefront of railway technology. Just as it had the first electrified inter-city main line of the 20th century it may, depending on timing, have the first newly electrified main line of the 21st. For on 14th July 2012 the government, after a 31 year wait, announced electrification of the Midland main line to Sheffield. Sheffield will also have the country's first tram-trains by 2015 when a pilot scheme will allow trams to transfer between their own tracks and the GC line to Rotherham. In the longer term will come a new High Speed line when the London-Birmingham HS2 is extended to Leeds, but history is to repeat itself because, like the North Midland's high speed line of the 1830s, it will miss Sheffield itself. The plan is that this one will go via Meadowhall.

Sheffield is still a great steel-making centre but its modern industry is less imposing. In post-industrial Britain the forges, scrap yards and engineering plants of the Don Valley have largely given way to retail parks, stadiums and hi-tech industries as the steel city builds on its other traditions of sport and innovation.

Caprotti Class 5 No. 44753 storms the 6.45am Paignton-Bradford through Brightside at around 60mph on Saturday 23rd June 1962. The River Don Works fills the background and the District Railway curves away behind the engine. *Robert Anderson*
During the 1960s modernisation, a new signal box replaced the old Midland one situated behind the third and fourth carriages. After less than a decade, it was abolished in 1973 and converted into a p. way cabin as Sheffield power box control extended northwards.

The 1937 LMS Sectional Appendix shows the Midland line from Wincobank to Bradway(which it lists in the Up direction) as signalled by Absolute Block except in Sheffield station where "No block or bell" was used. There was also no block signalling on the Up reception lines between Upwell St. and Grimesthorpe junctions. Signal boxes, with mileages from previous boxes, were at: Wincobank Sidings(signals arrival and departure lines only. 1614yds from Harrison & Camm's, Rotherham,) Wincobank North Jn.(161yds,) Wincobank Station Jn.(1094yds,) Brightside Station Jn.(984yds,) Upwell Street Jn.(585yds,) Grimesthorpe Jn. No.1(612yds,) Mill Race Junction(587yds,) Attercliffe Road(1617yds,) Nunnery Main Line Jn.(614yds,) Sheffield North Jn.(573yds,) Sheffield Station 'A'(signals Down lines only except No.5 platform line,) Sheffield Station 'B'(signals Up lines only including No.5 platform line) - both boxes 156yds from North Jn. Sheffield South No.1(Down lines only,) Sheffield South No.2(Up lines only) - both 253yds from 'A' and 'B' boxes, Queen's Road(1043yds,) Heeley Station(1072yds,) Heeley Carriage Sidings(840yds,) Millhouses & Ecclesall(1330yds,) Beauchief(1598yds,) Dore & Totley Station Jn.(1181yds,) Dore & Totley South Jn.(691yds.) Then 2 miles 50yds to Dronfield Colliery Sidings box. The gradient from Sheffield to Dore & Totley was almost constant at 1 in 100 rising.

Additional running lines were Up and Down Goods Harrison & Camm's-Brightside Station Jn., Down Goods and Up and Down Local lines Brightside Station Jn.-Mill Race Jn., Up and Down Local Sheffield Station South-Dore & Totley, and Down Goods Queen's Road-Heeley. An instruction was given that when passing over Attercliffe Viaduct the brakes of all vehicles should, as far as possible, be off. A 10mph speed restriction was in force on the 851yd curve from Wincobank Sidings to the Barnsley line.

The 1969 Eastern Region Appendix showed Track Circuit Block in force on the Up Main between Nunnery Main line Jn. and Wincobank Station Jn. with no intermediate signal boxes except the new Brightside Station Jn. The Down Goods line Heeley-Queen's Road had gone. Additional running lines north of Mill Race(now defined by signals controlled from Brightside Jn.) were now Up and Down Goods throughout to Harrison & Camm's with a mixture of Track Circuit and Permissive Block. The maximum line speed was given as 80mph on Main and Fast lines and 45mph on Goods lines.

The Wincobank North-Barnsley line curve was shown as Wincobank North Jn.-Wincobank Station Jn.(West Junction Points.) It was subject to a 20mph speed limit and worked as a siding.

Regularly seen from passing trains until the industrial collapse of the 1980s were the sidings that disappeared into the dark interiors of massive steel plants and the small industrial locos that worked them. Here, on Thursday 22nd July 1976, green-liveried Hudswell Clarke 0-4-0 diesel hydraulic, builders No. D816 built in 1954, stands by the British Steel Corporation's Grimesthorpe (Carlisle Street)Works. The engine still carries its original English Steel Corporation running number ESC No. 32 on a cabside plate. *S. Chapman*

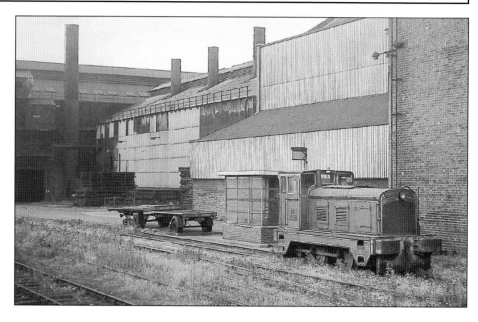

Working of hot ingots from works to works. When a request is received for the movement of hot ingots from Works to Works at Sheffield, the District Goods Manager must make the necessary arrangements locally in conjunction with the District Controller, the District Permanent Way Inspector and the District Carriage and Wagon Foreman, provided the hot ingots are loaded on suitable vehicles, are within gauge when loaded and do not exceed 80 tons in weight.

The ingots must be worked at a speed not exceeding 4 mph under careful supervision.

The road must be carefully examined before and after each movement, and the ingots must not be brought to a stand immediately beneath or closely adjoining any structures. When working hot ingots between 60 and 80 tons in weight from Messrs Cammell's Grimesthorpe Works to Messrs Vickers' Works and vice versa, all points must be clipped.

Hot ingots exceeding 80 tons in weight must be treated as exceptional loads and be dealt with in accordance with the regulations governing the movement of "Out of gauge and otherwise exceptional loads" .... *LMS 1937 Sectional Appendix.*

Above: Just so much scrap. Following closure of the Woodhead line, many of the Class 76(EM1) Bo-Bo electric locos were scrapped, ironically, on Midland territory at the yard of Cooper's Metals which was on the site of Cardigan Sidings, Grimesthorpe. Three members of the class being cut up when seen from a passing Sheffield-York train on Thursday 31st March 1983 included 76031 and 76032. Behind them is the original Sheffield & Rotherham line to Wicker while the large buildings to the left are the former Firth Brown Atlas Works, then in the course of partial demolition. *Stephen Chapman*

Below: Was this 1950s Locomotive Club of Great Britain railtour the first passenger train at Wicker since 1870? To the right of Millhouses ex-Midland 2P 4-4-0 No. 40487 is the great Cyclops Works, on the left is the goods yard's overhead crane, and in the distance the goods shed. *Peter Cookson collection*

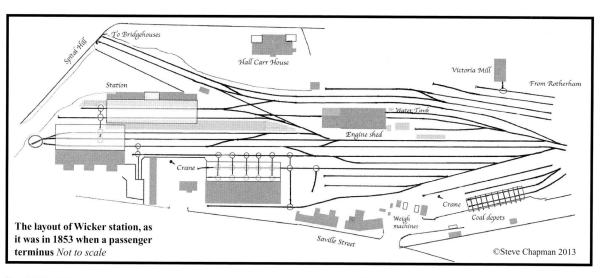

The layout of Wicker station, as it was in 1853 when a passenger terminus *Not to scale*

©Steve Chapman 2013

The LMS 1937 Sectional Appendix gave the following instructions for the working of trains over the incline to Bridgehouses via Spital Hill Tunnel:
When proceeding from Elevated signal box towards the LNE Railway, drivers must not exceed 12mph until after passing over Lockwood's Crossing. The number of vehicles taken up the incline at one time must be regulated in accordance with the state of the weather and the rails, so as to prevent the engine coming to a stand in the tunnel; not more than equal to 17 loads of mineral or more than 20 vehicles must be taken up the incline at one time. The guard or shunter must satisfy himself that all the vehicles are properly coupled together and attached to the engine, and that all brakes are released.

Drivers of trains ascending the incline must be careful not to suddenly check the speed when near the LNE end of the tunnel, in order to avoid breaking the couplings on the change of gradient near the mouth of the tunnel. Should a train ascending the incline come to a stand owing to the engine being unable to propel the train...and it is necessary to return to Lockwood's Crossing, to enable the engine to make another attempt.......the guard or shunter must satisfy himself that none of the vehicles have become uncoupled before the engine moves in the direction of Lockwood's Crossing, and apply wagon brakes if necessary.

Light engines or an engine and brake may be allowed to proceed from Lockwood's Crossing towards the LNE Railway without the signal fixed near Lockwood's Crossing and worked from the LNE end of the tunnel being taken off, and drivers of light engines or an engine and brake, may, when in possession of the Staff, pass the signal fixed near Lockwood's Crossing and worked from the LNE end, at danger, but must be careful to bring their engine or engines and brake to a stand clear of the swing scotch blocks...near the LNE end of the tunnel. All vehicles from Lockwood's Crossing to the LNE Railway must be propelled.

The signal fixed near Lockwood's Crossing, applicable to trains proceeding to the LNE, is worked by the LNE company's staff.

When descending the incline drivers must not exceed 12mph when proceeding from the LNE Railway to Lockwood's Crossing, and not more than equal to 29 loads of mineral or more than 30 vehicles must be taken down the incline at one time.

The guard or shunter must satisfy himself that all the vehicles about to be taken down the incline are properly coupled together and attached to the engine, and as the vehicles are drawn to the incline, must pin down a sufficient number of wagon brakes to enable the train to descend the incline at a speed not exceeding 12mph. The number of wagon brakes pinned down must not be less than one for every two heavily loaded, three lightly loaded, or four empty vehicles above eight. The brakes of loaded vehicles must, as far as possible, be used.

Wicker Goods Station was listed in the 1956 Handbook of Stations as having a maximum crane capacity of 35 tons and equipped to handle general goods, furniture vans, carriages, motor cars, portable engines and machines on wheels.

*The 1937 LMS Sectional Appendix listed the **Wicker branch** as 1900yds long from Lockwood's Crossing to Grimesthorpe Junction No.1. Signal boxes were: Lockwood's Crossing, Elevated Box(478yds from Lockwood's,) Firth's Sidings(466yds,) and Grimesthorpe Jn. No.2 (859yds.)*

Signalling was by Telegraph Bell to Firth's Sidings with 'No Block and Bell' Firth's Sidings-Grimesthorpe No.1. An additional main running line ran from Grimesthorpe No.2 to Firth's Sidings. When branch signal boxes were closed, a train could run if accompanied by a pilot guard wearing a red badge with "pilotman" in white letters. The summer 1963 working timetable showed Elevated and Firth's boxes as open 6am Monday-9.50pm Saturday, and Grimesthorpe No.2 5am Monday until Sunday's No.42trip(7.15am Engine Shed Sidings-Nunnery) was out of section.

The 1937 Appendix stated that wagons could be worked in both directions between Grimesthorpe and Wicker without a brake van on the rear.

Private Sidings served by the Wicker branch 1956
English Steel Corporation, Cyclops Works
English Steel Corporation, Grimesthorpe Works
Firth Brown Tools Ltd.(via Atlas Works)
Thos. Firth & John Brown, Atlas Blast Furnaces
Thos. Firth & John Brown Atlas Works
Thos. Firth & John Brown Midland Forge
Norfolk and East & West Gun Works
Norfolk Bar Treatment Shop
Kayser, Ellison & Co. Carlisle Works
Spear & Jackson, Etna Works
Sheffield Corporation Central Depot

Above: With the shed building and its large water tank in the background, LMS Hughes-Fowler "Crab" 2-6-0 No. 2761 stands by the ash plant in Grimesthorpe depot yard during the late 1940s. *Tom Greaves*

Dating from 1877, Grimesthorpe depot replaced a roundhouse on the opposite side of the main running lines which remained in use until about 1901, and which itself had replaced the two-road shed at Wicker in 1861. Mainly responsible for the supply of goods and mixed traffic locomotives, when under London Midland jurisdiction, Grimesthorpe motive power depot was 19A Sheffield and head of a district embracing sheds at Millhouses, Canklow and in LMS days even York South(19F.) Upon transfer to the Eastern Region it became Sheffield (Grimesthorpe) and was re-coded 41B - subordinate to Darnall.

Grimesthorpe lost its allocation at the end of 1961 and the shed was demolished in 1962 to make way for the new Sheffield Freight Terminal, but the site continued in use for a short time afterwards as a stabling point for main line diesel locomotives and shunters.

Below: Grimesthorpe shed will be remembered for its large allocation of 3F and 4F 0-6-0s. Plenty of 4Fs are in evidence on Sunday 30th April 1961 with Nos. 44477, 44174, 44437, 44547, 44212 and 44568 on show. The 1930's coaling plant towers over them.
John Beaumont/Robert Anderson archive

40

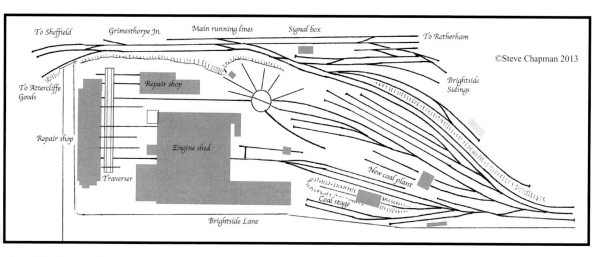

©Steve Chapman 2013

Above: The layout at Grimesthorpe motive power depot as it was in 1935 during remodelling, when the new mechanical coal and ash plants were under construction. *Not to scale.* Facilities at Grimesthorpe included a workshop added in 1898 with eight stalls connected by a traverser for the repair of engines throughout the 19 district. Inside the roundhouse was a single 46ft turntable, and outside a 60ft turntable installed in 1901 around which engines were stabled.

Locomotives allocated to Sheffield Grimesthorpe(41B) June 1961: Hughes-Fowler 'Crab' 2-6-0: 42794/97; Ivatt 4MT 2-6-0: 43089/146/60/1; Johnson 3F 0-6-0: 43254/637/69/751; Midland 4F 0-6-0: 43872; LMS 4F 0-6-0: 44174/212/65/87/426/37/77/547/68; LMS 3F 0-6-0T: 47548/624; 350hp 0-6-0 diesel: D3086/129/251-4/88/9/93/336/574/5/662/98/727/4028/9/35-44/6/7/8. Total: 52. Also based at Grimesthorpe was 45-ton steam breakdown crane No.102.

Below: One of the many and various 0-6-0s allocated to Grimesthorpe shed for local freight workings stands on one of the outdoor turntable roads during the transition from the LMS to British Railways in 1948. No. 58262 is an original of the 2F class designed by S. W. Johnson with larger 5ft 3 in driving wheels and introduced by the Midland Railway in 1878. On the right and still awaiting her BR number, 58151, is 22970, a Johnson 2F variant introduced in 1875 with 4ft 11 in driving wheels, and rebuilt with a Belpaire firebox in place of the round-topped type seen on 58262. *A. G. Ellis/Neville Stead collection*

41

Above: By the coal hopper while visiting Grimesthorpe is Toton 8F 2-8-0 No. 48007. *Tom Greaves*

Below: Johnson 1F 0-6-0T No. 1857 was a Grimesthorpe stalwart, surviving there well into the 1950s as BR No. 41857 and rebuilt with a Belpaire firebox since this picture was taken. *Tom Greaves*

On Sunday 3rd March 1963, Alex Scott noted the following on Grimesthorpe stabling point: Sulzer Type 4: D22/55; Sulzer Type 2: 7578; Brush Type 2: D5527/5639/85/89/5836/47/49; English Electric Type 1: D8050/52/55/57/58/59/64/65/69; 350hp 0-6-0: D3129/3336/3439/3727/4028/37/39/42/43/46/47. Total: 31

In summer 1963, Grimesthorpe stabling point had the following booked pilot duties: *No.16 Engine Shed Sidings:* yard shunting; *No.17 Cardigan Sidings:* yard shunting. Shunts Grimesthorpe Carriage & Wagon shops 5.30-8.30pm Monday-Saturday; *No.18 Wicker goods shed:* shed shunting; *No.21 Wicker Iron Yard:* Iron Yard shunting and shunts special traffic as required; *No.19 Attercliffe Yard:* yard shunting; *No.33 West Tinsley:* yard shunting; *No.22 Wincobank Down sidings:* yard shunting; *No.23 Wincobank Up sidings:* yard shunting.

Above: LNER D49 4-4-0 No. 238 *The Burton* simmers by the outdoor turntable having probably worked in with a service from Hull. Grimesthorpe would customarily service engines working in from the North Eastern. Grimesthorpe steel works darkens the background. *Neville Stead collection*

Class 5 4-6-0 No. 44805 heads past Nunnery Main Line Junction signal box with a 1950s class A passenger train departing from Sheffield Midland. Behind the signal box, the curve goes up to Nunnery sidings while the plate girder bridge carries the Wharf Street goods branch. Directly above that is the bridge carrying Navigation Hill. *Tom Greaves*

Right: In the depths of Nunnery Cutting, rebuilt Johnson 3F 0-6-0 No. 43749, of Grimesthorpe shed, plods beneath Victoria station's eastern approach lines with a northbound trip working during the 1950s. *Tom Greaves*

SHORT MEMORIES

December 1945: A exhibition at Victoria station celebrating the centenary of the Woodhead line's completion features such new locomotives as green B1 8304 *Gazelle,* L1 2-6-4T 9000 and Bo-Bo electric No. 6701.

6.10.47: B1 No. 1223 leaves Victoria on the inaugural Master Cutler driver by the Master Cutler R. A Balfour.

31.5.48: Low Moor Black Five No. 5101 brings the inaugural South Yorkshireman into Victoria. A B1 takes it forward.

Below: The signalman's view from Nunnery Main Line Junction box with Bescot(then 3A) 8F 2-8-0 No. 48766 passing beneath the Wharf Street branch as it heads light engine towards Grimesthorpe. *Tom Greaves*

Left: Also viewed from Nunnery Main Line Junction box in the 1950s, Jubilee 4-6-0 No. 45663 *Jervis* heads meaningfully towards Sheffield Midland with a Bradford to Bristol express. It has just passed under the stone bridge carrying the Nunnery Colliery Railway. *Tom Greaves*

SHORT MEMORIES

14.9.54: A4 No. 60008 works from King's Cross to Victoria in 2hrs 51mins with the official party for the electrification completion ceremony. The special is taken forward by EM2 No. 27000.

Below: Apologies to readers who have already seen this picture in Railway Memories No.21, but now it is in the correct book!
Sheffield may be memorable for Jubilees, B17s and EM2s but this must be its hidden treasure. On the Nunnery Colliery Railway(by then part of the National Coal Board) an 0-6-0T built by Kerr Stuart of Stoke-on-Trent, crosses the stone bridge in the previous picture with a load of coal and coke for the colliery's city coal yard in Blast Lane. *Tom Greaves*

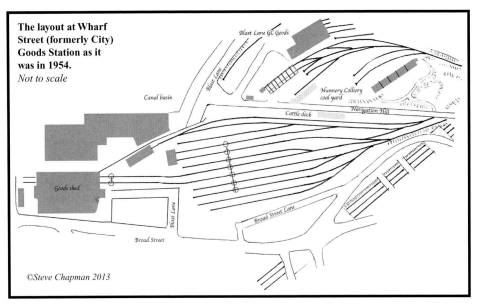

The layout at Wharf Street (formerly City) Goods Station as it was in 1954.
Not to scale

Blast Lane GC Goods

Canal basin

Nunnery Colliery coal yard

Cattle dock

Navigation Hill

Blast Lane

Goods shed

Blast Lane

Broad Street Lane

Broad Street

©Steve Chapman 2013

The former LNWR goods station was named Sheffield City until September 1950 when British Railways renamed it Wharf Street. The yard extended above Blast Lane with two sidings going into the first floor of the large three-storey warehouse. Two 20-ton hydraulic lifts lowered wagons to the ground level on Wharf Street. The 1956 Index of Stations listed it as having a maximum crane capacity of 10 tons and equipped to handle general goods. Wharf Street closed on 12th July 1965 but remained in use for private siding traffic into the 1970s.

The line between Nunnery Yard and City Station is worked by pilotman, and no train must be allowed to enter the section at either end unless accompanied by the pilotman.

When a train has been piloted from Nunnery Yard to City Station, the pilotman must remain in charge of such train until he has brought it back to Nunnery Yard.

Trains approaching the City Goods Station must be brought to a stand at the dwarf signal near the entrance to the City Station Yard until the pilotman has ascertained that all is clear. *LMS Sectional Appendix 1937.*

The pilotman wore on his left arm an armlet with red badge and "pilotman" in white letters.

The BR Eastern Region 1969 Sectional Appendix showed the by then Wharf Street Goods Station branch as being 1290yds long from the Nunnery Yard Shunter's cabin and worked according to One Engine in Steam regulations with a maximum speed of 15mph. The Token permitting access to the branch was kept at the Nunnery Yard Shunter's Cabin with the Shunter being the person authorised to give the Token to the driver and receive it upon return of the train.

One of Grimesthorpe's many 3F 0-6-0s, No. 43334, undertakes shunting duties at the entrance to Wharf Street yard on Thursday 21st June 1951. *Alan Ashley*

Nunnery Colliery branch: Drivers of trains to Nunnery Yard must bring their trains to a stand clear of the sidings until instructed by the shunter to proceed. Vehicles placed in Nunnery Colliery Sidings must be left on the main line side of the Woodbourne Road level crossing. *LMS Sectional Appendix 1937 and BR Eastern Region Sectional Appendix 1969.*

Above: At the top end of the Midland curve from Nunnery Main Line Junction in the mid-1950s, LMS-built 4P Compound 4-4-0 No. 41143, of 16A Nottingham shed, is at Nunnery carriage sidings with stock for a class B passenger train. The GC lines are clearly visible on the left. *Tom Greaves*

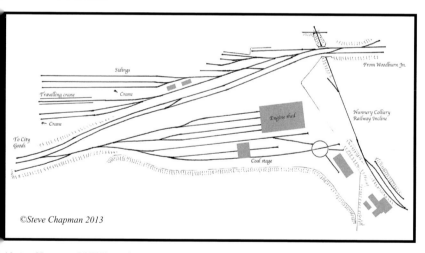

©Steve Chapman 2013

Above: Nunnery LNWR engine shed layout as it was in 1925. *Not to scale*

The LMS 1937 Sectional Appendix described the Nunnery Branch as being 691yds long from Nunnery Main Line Junction to Nunnery Single Line Junction, signalled by Absolute Block and with a rising gradient of 1 in 60.

The Eastern Region 1969 Sectional Appendix showed an almost different railway following the remodelling to restore the curve as a through route. It showed the line as 494yds long from Nunnery Main Line Junction to Sheffield Victoria No. 4, signalled by Track Circuit Block with a maximum speed of 20mph. Only the gradient hadn't changed. The 1969 Appendix also stated that only three passenger vehicles could be worked from Nunnery Sidings to Sheffield Station without a brake van on the rear, over the Up Main.

Above: The north end of Sheffield Midland in the early 1950s, gloriously soot-blackened on a dusty summer's day and overlooked by terraced houses now long gone. Kentish Town-based Stanier Class 5 4-6-0 No. 44846 emerges from the North tunnel, which marks the portal to Nunnery cutting, and rolls into the station with a southbound class A service. *Tom Greaves*

Below: This mouthwatering 1960 scene shows the north end of the station with the station buildings in the centre background. BR Standard Class 4 4-6-0 No. 75064 is at platform 2 and the unidentifiable Jubilee on platform 1. The time is believed to be around 10am and the trains are thought to be a Nottingham-Bradford and a Birmingham-Newcastle respectively. *Peter Cookson*

Above: Another BR Standard coming onto the scene at Sheffield in the early 1950s, Millhouses' own Class 5 4-6-0 No. 73014 looks to be removing its empty coaching stock to Nunnery sidings. Over on the right, Caprotti Stanier Class 5 No. 44754 has charge of a northbound named express which, judging by the lettering on the headboard, is the Thames-Clyde. *Tom Greaves*

The LMS 1937 Sectional Appendix stated: "...when it is necessary at the following stations for the fireman of a passenger train to go to the guard in order to obtain the journal of the run, the driver in clear weather only may move his engine as the station staff require whilst the fireman is absent.." Sheffield was one of a dozen stations listed.

Below: Among the veteran tank engines still to be seen at Sheffield in the 1950s were the ex-Lancashire & Yorkshire 2-4-2s which had a spell on Barnsley and Cudworth services. Royston's 50646 waits in the north end bay with such a service. *Neville Stead collection*

Above: Practically new Fairburn 2-6-4T No. 42145 of 20C Royston shed stands in one of the north end bay platforms with what is almost certainly a stopping service to Cudworth in around 1950. Meanwhile, the ex-Midland Railway condenser-fitted 1P 0-4-4T No. 1377, class dating from 1889, on pilot duty has yet to receive its BR number which will be 58071. The buildings above illustrate how houses and factories were once intermingled, long before the age of industrial and residential estates. *Tom Greaves*

Sheffield, Working at Station: The line alongside No. 1 platform line is named "First down middle line," and the line alongside No. 2 platform line is named "Second down middle line."

"All engines and vehicles must be stopped clear of the buffer stops on Nos. 3 and 4 platform lines.

"The connection between the shunting siding and the up fast line is provided for use by trains other than passenger trains. Passenger trains must not be passed through this connection except in the case of accident or obstruction." *LMS Sectional Appendix 1937*

The Appendix also stated that the maximum length of passenger or empty stock trains between Sheffield and Rotherham Westgate was 10 bogie vehicles or equivilant, presumably due to platform length at Westgate.

Below: Another of Millhouses shed's Johnson 1P 0-4-4 tanks on station pilot duty. No. 1396 was also from the batch introduced in 1889, all of which were subsequently rebuilt by Fowler with Belpaire fireboxes, except No.1377 which was destined to stay in original form and yet survive into the mid-1950s. No. 1396 would become BR No. 58076. *Neville Stead collection*

Above: On 6th April 1955, the 3.10pm express to Hull awaits departure behind D49/1 "Shire" 4-4-0 No. 62722 *Huntingdonshire* **of 53B Hull Botanic Gardens.** *B. G. Tweed/Peter Cookson collection*

Below: This view provides a splendid appreciation of the interior in the original part of the station with its once magnificent arched roof. Ivatt Class 4 2-6-0 No. 43037, a Canklow engine previously at Grimesthorpe, has charge of what may well be a service running between Rotherham and the Hope Valley. *Tom Greaves*

Above: Class 2P 4-4-0 No. 40491, from 18C Hasland shed, is bathed in dappled sunlight while inside the original covered part of the station c1950, about the time when the station was named Sheffield City. The trainshed roof was removed and replaced by canopies in 1956/57. *Tom Greaves*

Below: In the later extended portion of the station, Compound 4-4-0 No. 41137 of Leeds Holbeck is on the First Down Middle line with empty fish vans for Fleetwood during the 1950s. *Tom Greaves*

Above: Stanier Class 5 4-6-0 No. 44888 and Jubilee No. 45562 *Alberta* pull into platform 1 with the 12-coach down Devonian, formed of Western Region chocolate and cream stock, at 4.52pm on Saturday 19th May 1962. *Robert Anderson*

Below: Nowadays, full headlights are compulsory on locomotives in order to ensure good visibility of approaching trains but in the mid-1960s the idea was a new innovation, even then it took more than 20 years to be adopted as standard in place of the less powerful marker lights. Finsbury Park's Brush Type 4 No. D1509, at platform 1 with the afternoon Pullman to King's Cross, is fitted with experimental headlights. The trials, which tested Lucas amber foglamps as well as clear and flashing lamps, were aimed at eliminating such problems as headcodes being rendered difficult to read, and any hypnotic affect on drivers able to see the sleepers flashing beneath them at speed. A cravens-built DMU stands at the south end of platform 2. *Tom Greaves*

Above: The final indignity - redundant Woodhead line electrics paraded at Sheffield Midland. On the afternoon of Thursday 24th November 1983 this sad ensemble was waiting on the Second Down Middle line as BR/Sulzer Type 2 No. 25221 delivered EM1s Nos. 76002, 48, 50 and 43 to their doom at Cooper's Metals.

Left: Misfortune struck "Peak" No. 46031 while working the Leeds to Poole service on 13th May 1982, and it is seen at platform 1 after being hauled in by 45063.

Bottom: Favoured station pilot in the 1980s was Tinsley depot's 350hp 0-6-0 shunter No. 08691 which had been spruced up and named *Escafeld*, the old English name for Sheffield. She is seen here dealing with vans at the south end of platform 6 on Thursday 1st October 1987.
All Stephen Chapman

Above: The exterior of Sheffield Midland station in the 1950s. While buses gather, the station is dwarfed by the church and rows of begrimed terraced houses on Park Hill. In the next decade the houses would be replaced by the Park Hill flats, an iconic symbol of 1960s Sheffield. *Tom Greaves*

The ornate station frontage and buildings came with the station extension and were added in 1904. Designed by Charles Trubshaw, they were criticised at the time for their lack of stature and such grand features as a clocktower and an overall roof.

Below: The many and varied locomotives once seen at Sheffield Midland included unrebuilt Patriot 4-6-0s from Bristol Barrow Road shed which were regulars on North East-South West expresses south of York. A Jubilee looks on as No. 45519 *Lady Godiva* pulls out of platform 5 with the 7.25am York-Bristol at 9.19am on Saturday 23rd July 1960. *John Beaumont/Robert Anderson archive*

Above: Premier motive power on the Midland line services during the later steam era was arguably the Royal Scot 7P 4-6-0s. No. 46113 *Cameronian* of Leeds Holbeck is at platform 8 with a St. Pancras express on 3rd September 1960. *Peter Cookson*

Below: More Class 7 power but this time in the shape of a less common Britannia Pacific. Holbeck shed turned out No. 70044 *Earl Haig* for the 12 o'clock Bradford Forster Square-St. Pancras when the booked diesel wasn't available on Saturday 19th May 1962. Delayed by the need to take water, it departs from platform 8 at 2pm. *Robert Anderson*

Above: The Great Central main line had lost most of its expresses but there were still various intermediate and local services, and some provided work for Darnall's remaining 'Large Director' 4-4-0s in their final summer. A somewhat bedraggled D11/1 No. 62660 *Butler Henderson* departs Killamarsh Central with the 4.20pm Sheffield Victoria-Nottingham Victoria stopping service in September 1960. Thankfully, 62660 has survived into preservation. *A. Drake/Colour-Rail*

Below: B17/6 4-6-0 No. 61641 *Gayton Hall* makes use of the turntable at the east end of Sheffield Victoria station in September 1958. *P. J. Hughes/Colour-Rail*

Volcanic departures by Eastern engines taking a run at the 1 in 100 climb ahead.
Above: Deputising for an errant diesel, York V2 2-6-2 No. 60842 raises a good head of steam while preparing to restart the 12.43pm Newcastle-Bristol from platform 6 on Saturday 2nd June 1962. *John Beaumont/Robert Anderson archive*

Below: Crusted in grime but at least steam-tight, Canklow B1 4-6-0 No. 61093 sets off from platform 5 with the 12.51 to Chinley on Saturday 17th March 1962. *Robert Anderson*

Above: A c1965 scene at the south end of the original part of the station where a Victorian gas lamp has survived the many changes occurring over the previous decade. Buxton's Ivatt Class 2 2-6-0 No. 46485 gets a Hope Valley stopping train on the move from platform 7 as a BR/Sulzer Type 2(Class 25) stands at platform 6. *This and the picture below: Tom Greaves*

Below: Sheffield South No. 2 signal box is the setting for LMS Stanier Class 3P 2-6-2T No. 82 as she departs for Millhouses shed during the transition to British Railways. The Black Five in the background has its LMS number, 4820, but British Railways on the tender.

Above: First of the much admired 2,500hp Class EM2 Co-Co express passenger locos, No. 27000, at the east end of Sheffield Victoria station in September 1958. Green livery has replaced the original black but she has yet to receive her name *Electra*. From 1959 the EM2s and EM1s 26046-57 were given the names of characters from antiquity. *Geoff Warnes/Colour-Rail*

Below: Also at Victoria station, Doncaster B1 4-6-0 No. 61158 in platform 3 on Saturday 29th August 1964. *Colour-Rail*

Above: An unidentified Class 76 Bo-Bo rolls a Manchester-Sheffield service down-grade through a chilly landscape and past Dughty Bridge signal box on Saturday 3rd January 1970. *Robert Anderson*

Below: The general view of Brown Bayley's works at Attercliffe on Saturday 26th February 1977. The GC Woodburn Junction-Mexborough line, electrified to Tinsley Yard, is in the foreground along with the Sheffield & Tinsley canal. The 0-4-0 saddletank is No. 7 Hudswell Clarke 1689, built in 1937. In 1973, Brown Bayley's had three 0-4-0STs, two Hudswell Clarkes and 1894-built Nasmyth Wilson 454 as well as three diesels. No. 7 is seen here following restoration for a new life in preservation. Brown Bayley Steels Ltd. was taken over by Hadfields but by 1984 the works was closed and being stripped, with some of it shipped to Turkey. The Don Valley Stadium was built on the site and at the time of writing, Sheffield City Council was even considering closing and demolishing the stadium in order to save money. *Stephen Chapman*

Above: At the south end of the later part of the station in about 1950, Hasland's 2P 4-4-0 No. 40491 reverses into platform 1 while running round its Chesterfield train. The lines between 40491 and the gas cylinders lead into Pond Street goods yard. *Tom Greaves*

Below: Jubilee No. 45694 *Bellerophon* brings the 500-ton Devonian unaided into Midland station only nine minutes late while deputising for a yet another failed diesel on Saturday 2nd June 1962. On the right are the station sidings and fish dock. *Robert Anderson*

Drivers must not bring their trains to a stand with the engine beneath the steps of the overbridge at the south end of No. 1 platform, except where necessary for the purpose of taking water.

When taking water at the column adjacent to the overbridge, every effort must be made to avoid engines blowing off steam and emitting smoke. *BR Eastern Region Sectional Appendix 1969.*

Above: Having used the turntable in the sidings at the south end of Midland station, Holbeck Jubilee No. 45739 *Ulster* stands ready for its return working at 9.20am on Saturday 24th November 1962. This facility was especially useful for turning engines working in from Leeds in the latter years of steam when no other facilities were available nearby. The site is no less important nowadays following the construction of a new servicing shed for diesel units in 1988. *Robert Anderson*

On the left is the loading dock which later saw use as a Motorail terminal. Besides being a passenger station, Sheffield Midland was also listed in the 1956 Handbook of Stations as equipped to handle horse boxes and prize cattle vans, and carriages and motor cars by passenger or parcels train.

Below: Midland station seen from Shrewsbury Road on Wednesday 3rd January 2001 as Metro-Cammell DMU No. 101682 leaves platform 2A on the 12.14 stopping service to Manchester Picadilly. The power signal box, commissioned over the weekend Saturday 20th/Sunday 21st January 1973 is on the left, as is platform 1. Towering behind it is the 9-storey Sheaf House built on the site of Pond Street goods yard in the mid-1960s. Accommodating the divisional manager's, civil engineer's and signal & telecommunications engineer's organisations as well as the BT Police, it was once voted Britain's second ugliest building - after Northampton bus station. The Sheffield divisional manager's organisation was disbanded in 1983 and its territory shared between Leeds and Doncaster. It is interesting that when the office block was ultimately vacated, little time was wasted in demolishing it. *Stephen Chapman*

Left: Brightside station, closed since May 1995 but with lights and shelters still intact on 3rd April 2002 when Brush Type 4 No. 47831 *Bolton Wanderer* was heading a Birmingham-Newcastle Virgin Cross-Country service.

Notice the clean buildings in the background and the lack of towering steel plants and furnaces, only the Sheffield Forgemasters' River Don works remaining on the left.

Centre: One of those plants gone from the above scene is the Grimesthorpe Works. This 0-4-0 diesel hydraulic built by the North British Locomotive Co. for the then English Steel Corporation in 1959, was seen from a passing train in 1974.

Below: The time-honoured Newcastle-Bristol mail served Sheffield Midland en-route. Ex-ScotRail Brush 4 No. 47706 has left the train in platform 6 while collecting vans from platform 7 on Thursday 14th April 1994. The Sheffield stop was replaced by a new mail terminal at Doncaster shortly afterwards but since 2004 mail trains have run only between London, Warrington and Glasgow.

All Stephen Chapman

On 12th March 1979 the 08.17 from Chesterfield(2J55,) a Class 123 DMU, cars 52102, 59826 and 52093, ran away approaching Sheffield and collided at 20-25mph with an empty 2-car Class 108 set on train 1D62 which had failed in platform 1. But for the actions of the 123's crew and a driver travelling passenger in applying hand brakes to reduce the speed from 70mph, and moving passengers from the front of the train, the result could have been tragic. Only six passengers were injured and none kept in hospital.

Driver J. Graveling told the inquiry that followed that upon passing Heeley Carriage Sidings he made his usual brake application and heard the air rushing in but there was no application of the brake blocks and speed was not appreciably reduced. Without placing the handle to the "Lap" position, he looked at the duplex gauge which showed 10in of vacuum in the train pipe and 28-30in. on the high vacuum side. As the brake application was having no effect he brought the brake handle round to the "On" position; still nothing happened. He turned to driver J. Briddon in the assistant's seat(outside the cab) and said: " Jeff. We are not stopping. There's no brake." Driver Briddon looked in the cab and saw the speedometer

Class 108(right) and 123 DMUs at Sheffield Midland on Saturday 10th November 1979.

showing 65mph. He replied: "Put it in first gear and put the handbrake on. I'll get back." Having released the DSD, driver Graveling was unable to engage first gear so he applied the handbrake as tightly as he could and then sounded the horn as far as the last bridge approaching Sheffield at which point he evacuated the cab. He entered the leading compartment and shouted at the passengers: "Get out quickly. We're going to crash!" He was half way along the leading vehicle when the collision occurred. Driver Briddon, meanwhile, was running to the rear cab to apply the handbrake there when the crash happened.

On hearing the 123's emergency horn, the power box staff gave 1D62 a clear signal in an attempt to move it away and called the emergency services.

The rear car of 1D62(51923) was almost totally destroyed when the heavier 52102 over-rode it while 52102 was also badly damaged and its bogie displaced.

Above: Near Farm Road, Ivatt Class 2 2-6-0 No. 46465 climbs out of Sheffield Midland with a Hope Valley service during the mid-1960s. The Up Fast line to Chesterfield and beyond is on the right while the Down Fast is in the underpass cutting on the left. The north portal of the underpass is decorated by a stone carving of the Midland Railway wyvern above the arch, a feature still visible in 2013. The line to Dore & Totley reverted to two tracks in 1971/72 but for a Down Loop from Queen's Road to Sheffield and an Up Loop from Heeley to Millhouses. The underpass was abandoned but the Sheffield end of the line was retained with a carriage washer. *Tom Greaves*

Above: Again on Hope Valley duty, Ivatt Class 2 2-6-0 No. 46465 passes Queen's Road during the mid-1960s. The underpass for the Down Fast line is bottom right while in the background are the remains of Queen's Road goods depot which closed on 13th May 1963. The goods shed and cattle dock are still there but the track had been removed save for the few carriage sidings. The 1956 Handbook of Stations listed Queen's Road as having a 5-ton crane capacity and equipped to handle general goods and livestock. *Tom Greaves*

Below: With steam to spare, Bristol Barrow Road Jubilee No. 45570 *New Zealand* rolls an express from the South West down to Sheffield and over the River Sheaf in early BR days. Millhouses shed is in the right background and Victoria Works, which made automotive components, on the left. *Tom Greaves*

Tom Greaves, Sheffield Division traction engineer during the early 1960s, recalls: "Grimesthorpe shed was running down when I went there. Its most important part was the big pumphouse. The water pump fed all the Midland side of Sheffield, and Canklow. "The shed had a really good workshop with a very proficient maintenance team who in my experience were always ready to take on the challenge of something different, like Midland compounds and Caprotti Class 5s. Don Cowan and Ken Pitts were two of the team. Don became first depot manager at Tinsley - a very good engineer.

"Millhouses shed was small and select, covering top link passenger and providing passenger tanks for the semi-fasts, such as to Chinley, and station pilots.

"When Darnall was being run-down prior to Tinsley opening, it became the recipient of LM locos such as Royal Scots and Jubilees. We thought of Darnall as a joint depot with Staveley GC. The shedmaster when I first arrived was Arthur Porter. The enginemen's lodge was moved there from Grimesthorpe. It was under the strict management of a formidable lady we called Big Mary and included a very good canteen. One day, the Eastern Region's Chief Mechanical & Electrical Engineer Colin Scutt, once a Darnall shedmaster, came to do an inspection. If the CM&EE was coming you set your stall out ready. David Scott, the running and maintenance engineer briefed everyone as to what they should do and to be at their best. The inspection went very well and we were on a high. Just as C.S. came out of the shed, who should appear from the canteen but Big Mary. She headed straight for him saying: "Colin lad, how lovely to see you" and with that she put her arms round his neck and pulled him into her ample bosom." We were all ordered not to laugh at seeing the boss robbed of his managerial dignity.

"There was a lot of adverse reaction from the staff at having to travel to Tinsley so a bus was put on for them. After three years we found that it would have been cheaper to buy each one of them a car. Tinsley Yard floated on a bed of oil from the Dowty retarders which at that time were constantly leaking.

"During my time in Sheffield we were based at The Farm - a beautiful building. When you walked inside there was no mistake you were in a stately home. Most of the ornate fittings had gone but beautiful cornices and architraves remained. Two floors were occupied - by the admin, the divisional manager's office and the commercial departments. The operating and motive power departments were outside in up-market 'Portakabins.' The whole place was driven by Stanley Webb, the Divisional Manager and an ardent LM man. In those days there was definitely a divide between the cultural and commercial departments and the "doing" part - the operations and motive power. A degree of factionism still survived between the Midland and GC sides - the greatest loyalty to the old railway was undoubtably among the GC people.

"Often forgotten is that Sheffield had three road motor depots, Norfolk Park being the biggest on the Eastern Region.

"The GC Rotherham branch was known as The Backbone of England because trains were block on block from Woodburn Junction to Mexborough. You could have two shifts relieving between Woodburn and Doncaster. But there was wonderful co-operation between the signalmen and the motive power. Tinsley Junction was one of the core boxes. Most freights were WD-hauled and some signalmen were very cautious about headways; they could hold a freight for ages. After Tinsley there wasn't anywhere else much to recess a freight until Mexborough so you didn't want an express following a freight clanking along at 15mph through one of the yellow fogs we used to get. One driver was called "Clogger Bell;" if he was on the freight they'd let him go ahead of an express because they knew it couldn't catch Clogger."

The shunter waits, pole in hand, for Ivatt Class 2 2-6-0 No. 46451 to pass on a Sheffield-bound train before operations at Millhouses goods yard can continue with 3F 0-6-0 No. 43174. The goods depot, on the right, was listed in the 1956 Handbook of Stations as having a 1 ton 10 cwt crane capacity and equipped to handle general goods. It did not close completely when Sheffield Freight Terminal opened, continuing to handle coal until April 1972. *Neville Stead*

The 1937 LMS Sectional Appendix stated that traffic for Laycock's engineering works siding must be worked "to or from Millhouses goods yard through the connection at the south end of Laycock's siding, a brake van in all cases to be at the Sheffield end when the wagons are being worked across the main line."

Above: The former Midland Railway Millhouses engine shed around 1950 when still firmly in LM hands. Johnson 2F 0-6-0 No. 58209(a rebuilt with a Belpaire firebox) simmers alongside LMS-built 4F 0-6-0 No. 44588. Jubilee No. 45664 *Nelson* is just inside the shed. *Tom Greaves*

Below: Visiting 4F 0-6-0 No. 44125 stands by the coal stage. *P. J. Hughes/Colour-Rail*

Hiding at the back of Millhouses shed on 23rd July 1960 was Compound 4-4-0 No. 40907. She would steam again on 21st August to be the last Compound in regular service. On 16th September she made her final run, to Doncaster for scrap. *Robert Anderson*

Opened in 1901, Millhouses shed mainly provided passenger engines for everything from top link expresses to station pilots and was thus home to some of the Midland Lines' finest engines as well as the most antique passenger tanks. It was coded 19B until transfer to the Eastern Region in 1958 saw it become 41C, subordinate to the former LNER depot at Darnall. The Sheffield district depots were soon rationalised after this event, especially with the Midland line being dieselised, and Millhouses succumbed on 1st January 1962. The shed survived in private industrial use for many years afterwards and still stood, derelict, in 2012; a Tesco car park occupies the yard.

Locomotives allocated to 19B Millhouses, September 1950: 3P 2-6-2T: 40139; Midland 2P 4-4-0: 40487/93/502/18/49; Midland 4P Compound 4-4-0: 41014/6/21/37; LMS 4P Compound 4-4-0: 41062/72/9; 2MT 2-6-2T: 41245/6; 3F 0-6-0: 43341; 5MT 4-6-0: 44664/5/859/962/3/4/5/86/5260/4/97; Jubilee 4-6-0: 45590 *Travancore*/45594 *Bhopal*/45607 *Fiji*/45621 *Northern Rhodesia*/45664 *Nelson*/45679 *Armada*/45683 *Hogue*/45725 *Repulse*; 1P 0-4-4T: 58067/8/71/6; 2F 0-6-0: 58209. Total: 40

Locomotives allocated to 41C Millhouses, June 1961: 2MT 2-6-2T: 41209/45/6; 4MT 2-6-0: 43032/7; Rebuilt Patriot 4-6-0: 45536 *Private W. Wood VC;* Jubilee 4-6-0: 45570 *New Zealand*/45576 *Bombay*/45590 *Travancore*/45594 *Bhopal*/45602 *British Honduras*/45607 *Fiji*/45627 *Sierra Leone*/45654 *Hood*/45656 *Cochrane*/45664 *Nelson*/45683 *Hogue*/45725 *Repulse;* Royal Scot 4-6-0: 46131 *The Royal Warwickshire Regiment*/46147 *The Northamptonshire Regiment*/46148 *The Manchester Regiment*/46151 *The Royal Horse Guardsman*/46164 *The Artists' Rifleman;* 2MT 2-6-0: 46400/50/1; 5MT 4-6-0: 73016/65/155; 2MT 2-6-0: 78022/3/4/5. Total: 33

Below: Millhouses motive power depot and goods yard in 1952 *Not to scale*

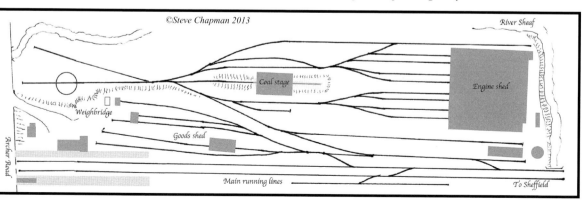

©Steve Chapman 2013

Left: In store, Midland 1P 0-4-4T LMS No. 1396 as rebuilt with Belpaire firebox. She was allotted BR number 58076. *Tom Greaves*

Below: One of the LMS-built Class 4P Compound 4-4-0s allocated to Millhouses, No 41062, rests on shed in c1952. These were prime Midland main line power until the Jubilees came along.
P. Tait/Peter Cookson colln.

Bottom: Stanier Class 5 4-6-0 No. 45139 arrives at the Millhouses & Ecclesall Down Local platform with a class 2 passenger service for Sheffield in July 1963.
Colour-Rail

SHORT MEMORIES

15.9.58: D207 works the inaugural Master Cutler Pullman to King's Cross.

19 & 20.9.58: W1 4-6-4 No. 60700 arrives at Victoria with the 6.40am from Doncaster, returning light engine.

12.7.59: D11s 62667 *Somme* and 62670 *Marne* noted on Sheffield-Cleethorpes extras. At least six of the class reported to be out of store for the summer.

January 1960: Compound 40907 regularly employed on 7.5am Sheffield-Chinley

15.1.60: The 7.40am Bristol-Bradford reaches Sheffield 30 mins. late with 40907 assisting Patriot 45504. Next day the train arrives 50 minutes late with 40907 assisting a Standard class 5 4-6-0.

Above: Working hard up the 1 in 100, Holbeck Jubilee No. 45569 *Tasmania* roars past Millhouses & Ecclesall station with the 12 o'clock Bradford-St. Pancras at 1.55pm on Tuesday 12th June 1962 while deputising for a diesel. The signal box is just visible towards the back end of the train while a 350hp diesel shunter(Class 08) shunts the station goods yard. *Robert Anderson*

Below: The going-away shot of the above picture gives a good view of the island platform, its building and fittings at Millhouses & Ecclesall station. The train is passing through the Up Fast platform; the left face of the island platform is on the Down Fast, the right face on the Up Local and the far right platform on the Down Local. Three versions of the station's name had been used during its time, the final one since 1932. Millhouses & Ecclesall closed to passengers on 10th June 1968. *Robert Anderson*

Above: The film has suffered damage but even so this is a well worthwhile view looking north from the footbridge at Dore & Totley station around the time of nationalisation. Dore & Totley Station Junction signal box is in the centre of the picture as Hasland 2P 4-4-0 No. 40557, still with LMS on her tender, arrives on a stopping train for Chesterfield. The signal box was abolished in June 1973 when Sheffield power box control was extended to interface with Tapton Junction and Totley Tunnel East. Nowadays only the platform on the left remains, served by a single line, the island platform being removed in 1985, allowing the main line curve to be eased.

Below: Millhouses' newly delivered Class 2 2-6-2T No. 41246 runs into the Hope Valley platform at Dore & Totley with a stopping service to Chinley in around 1951. *This picture by Alan Ashley. Picture above by Tom Greaves*

Above: Darnall B1 No. 61050 pulls out of Dore & Totley with the 12.45pm Sheffield-Chinley on Saturday 20th July 1963. Darnall was about to lose its steam allocation and 61050 would move to Canklow. *John Beaumont/Robert Anderson archive*

Below: Dore & Totley West Junction and signal box as seen from an inspection saloon in the 1960s. The line to Sheffield goes straight ahead and the curve to Dore South turns right behind the box. This box and Dore South were abolished in 1972 and replaced by a temporary panel in Dore & Totley station box pending transfer to Sheffield power box. *Tom Greaves*

SHORT MEMORIES

18.1.60: A4 Pacific 60015 *Quicksilver* arrives at Wadsley Bridge with a football special from King's Cross conveying Arsenal supporters.

1.2.60: Millhouses express passenger diagrams rostered for class 7 power. Five Class 5 4-6-0s replaced by Royal Scots and rebuilt Patriots. No. 46147 arrives at Midland on the 6.30am ex-Derby with a 5A shedplate but by the time it works the 1.57pm to St. Pancras it has a 41C shedplate.

26.5.60: Withdrawn WR 2-8-0s 2840/78/80 and 2-6-0 5319 hauled to a Killamarsh scrapyard for cutting up.

Above: The likelihood of today's youngsters eagerly watching the trains go by at Dore & Totley - or anywhere else - is very small indeed but then there isn't usually anything like this to inspire them.

Jubilees often needed the assistance of Compound 4-4-0s on Midland main line expresses, though judging by the LNER coach behind 45664 *Nelson* this is a South West to North East express. *Tom Greaves*

Below: Cricklewood's BR Standard Class 5 4-6-0 No. 73066 lays a smoke screen as she blasts an Up relief train through Dore & Totley on Saturday 20th July 1963. *John Beaumont/Robert Anderson archive*

Above: Having just passed Dore & Totley South Junction, Jubilee No. 45676 *Codrington* relaxes on the downhill run to Sheffield with a long summer relief from the West Country on Saturday 20th July 1963. *John Beaumont/Robert Anderson archive*

Below: After being held at the signal for trains to pass each way on the main line, an ex-LNWR 'Super D' 0-8-0 - probably a Buxton engine - starts to move over Dore & Totley South Junction and off the curve from Dore & Totley West. *Tom Greaves*
This curve allows trains to run direct between the Hope Valley line, Chesterfield and beyond and has at various times since the 1960s been used by St. Pancras-Manchester expresses. Nowadays it is single track but still carries substantial freight between the quarries and cement works of the Peak District and the south.

Left: The summer Saturday Bradford Exchange-Poole, worked by Holbeck Jubilees as far as Nottingham and back in the mid-1960s, will live on in railway folklore at least as long as those who witnessed this late steam era spectacle.

No. 45562 *Alberta*, bearing the yellow stripe forbidding her from working under the AC overhead electrified lines south of Crewe - but not the DC wires through Penistone - is about to plunge the train into Bradway Tunnel. *Tom Greaves*

Below: Shortly after completion of the Woodhead line electrification at 1500 volts DC, an EM1 class Bo-Bo and its Manchester-bound express emerge from the new Woodhead Tunnel and pass through the new Woodhead station. The disused track is still in situ through the old tunnels on the left where in 2012 a narrow gauge line still passed. The platforms were still in place in 2012 but the standard gauge track was long gone, the site being occupied by construction works involved in laying a National Grid cable through the 'new' tunnel.
Tom Greaves

THE GREAT CENTRAL LINES

BEWARE OF TRAINS

The scene at Dunford Bridge on Wednesday 3rd September 1980.
Above: Class EM1 Bo-Bos(Class 76 since 1968) Nos. 76029 and 76011 pass the station and West signal box with empty unfitted 21-ton hopper wagons returning east. By this time the line was carrying only 40 trains a day out of the 120 it could accommodate. By today's standards, 40 freights a day on any route is a lot! *Adrian Booth*

Below: An air-braked merry-go-round coal train bound for Fiddlers Ferry power station approaches Dunford Bridge behind 76034 and 76032. The sidings on the right are a reminder that there were once sorting yards here. *Adrian Booth*

EM1 No. E26017 passes Bullhouse with an eastbound class 8 train formed of 21-ton hoppers on Saturday 30th December 1967. The colliery sidings were on the left. *Adrian Booth*

The GC line from Beighton Junction to Woodhead was shown in the BR Eastern Region 1969 Sectional Appendix as signalled by Absolute Block from Beighton to Woodburn Jn., Track Circuit Block from Woodburn Jn. to Sheffield Victoria No. 4, Permissive Block Sheffield Victoria No. 4 to No. 3, Absolute Block Sheffield Victoria No. 3 to Woodhead but with Permissive Block between Sheffield No. 3 and No. 1 for trains not conveying passengers.

Signal boxes(with distance from previous box) were at: Beighton Junction, Holbrook Colliery Sidings(401yds,) Beighton Station Junction(570yds,) Woodhouse East Junction (1536yds,) Woodhouse West Junction(668yds,) Rotherwood(830yds,) Orgreaves Colliery(1190yds,) Handsworth Colliery(1329yds,) Darnall East(1583yds,) Darnall West (732yds,) Woodburn Junction(1231yds,) Sheffield Victoria No. 4(1559yds,) Sheffield Victoria No. 3(413yds,) Sheffield Victoria No. 1(1258yds,) Neepsend(660yds,) Wadsley Bridge(1 mile 1183yds,) Oughty Bridge(2 miles 315yds,) Wharncliffe Wood(1 mile 1065yds,) Deepcar(1 mile 405yds,)Wortley(1516yds,) Blackmoor Crossing(2 miles 456yds,) Willey Bridge Junction(1488yds,) Barnsley Junction(773yds,) Huddersfield Junction(962yds,) Penistone Goods(1322yds,) Thurlstone(1243yds,) Bullhouse(1 mile 232yds,) Hazlehead(1 mile 692yds,) Dunford East(936yds,) Dunford West(1 mile 1113yds,) Woodhead(3 miles 521yds.)

Additional running lines(signalled by Permissive Block unless otherwise stated) were: Woodhouse East-Sheffield Victoria No. 3(Up and Down Goods,) Down Goods Woodburn Junction-Sheffield Victoria No. 4(Track Circuit Block Permissive,) Up and Down platform lines Victoria station(Permissive Block,) Sheffield Victoria No. 1-Neepsend(Up Goods,) Wharncliffe Wood-Deepcar(Up and Down Goods,)Willey Bridge Junction-Huddersfield Junction(2x Up and Down Goods, No Block on one Down Goods,) Huddersfield Junction-Penistone Goods(Up Goods,) Thurlstone Crossing-Bullhouse Colliery(Down Goods,) Dunford East-West(Up Goods.) A Down Refuge Siding with standage for 50 wagons, engine and brake van was at Penistone Goods, and a Down Goods Loop with standage for 138 wagons, engine and brake at Dunford West. The maximum line speed was 60mph on main and fast lines and on slow and goods lines Bullhouse Colliery-Woodhead, but 30mph Beighton Junction-Woodhouse East.

An instruction was given that "a locomotive and not more than two brake vans" may be used to assist in the rear of a freight train between Woodburn Junction and Dunford Bridge and that the assisting locomotive must not be coupled to the train. The same applied from Woodhouse East Junction to Darnall East.

Above: 76031 and 76034 head a westbound freight past Penistone Goods on 11th July 1979.
Adrian Booth
Penistone was listed in the 1956 Stations Handbook as having a 5-ton crane capacity and equipped to deal with general goods, furniture vans, carriages, motor cars, portable engines and machines on wheels, livestock, horse boxes and prize cattle vans, and carriages and motor cars by passenger or parcels train.

Centre: EM1 No. 26048 rests in the sidings behind the Down side of Penistone station in the early 1950s. At this time, electrification was complete only between Wath and Dunford Bridge.
Tom Greaves

Bottom: Huddersfield Junction and Penistone station - stripped to the bare essentials with all passenger cover removed from the GC side - as seen on 19th August 1980 from the cab of 76003 on a Rotherwood-Garston coal train. The only passenger trains calling there turn right to Huddersfield.
Stephen Chapman

Above: EM1 No. 26043 crosses Huddersfield Junction at the head of the 12.25pm Frodingham-Mottram class 8 goods, consisting mainly of steel traffic, at 6.27pm on Saturday 24th August 1963. The EM1s had a noticeably different look to the EM2s, not least because their buffers and draw gear were mounted on the bogies whereas the on the EM2s they were fixed to the main frames. *Robert Anderson*

Below: The rerailing gang dealing with miscreant "covhops" stand back as EM2 No. E27006 *Pandora* and her express from Manchester creep cautiously past. It is the 1960s and *Pandora* is in newly applied blue livery but has yet to receive her yellow panel. Following closure of Gorton Works in 1963, the EM2s were overhauled at Crewe and consequently emerged in the electric blue applied to Crewe's own AC electrics. No. 27002 was first to be outshopped in the new livery with 27004 and 27006 following. But with the Woodhead line passenger service doomed, the EM2s would not remain in BR service that much longer, being placed in store by March 1968 and withdrawn in October. Worthy of better than scrap, they were sold to the Netherlands Railways where they enjoyed a new lease of life.
Tom Greaves.

Above: The scene at Barnsley Junction in the 1960s where EM1 No. 26044 stands with 16-ton mineral wagons. The lines from Sheffield come in on the extreme right while those to Wath and Barnsley curve to the left behind the EM1 standing light engine. The expanse of Barnsley Junction yard is behind 26044. Nowadays, there is nothing more than a single line through here forming part of the route from Barnsley to Huddersfield. *Tom Greaves*

Below: Steam still had a presence between Penistone and Sheffield and in this view Jubilee No. 45562 *Alberta* climbs the 1 in 120 through Deepcar with the 10.34am Bournemouth-Bradford Exchange at 6.59pm on 11th July 1964. The goods shed can be glimpsed in the right distance while the connection to the Stocksbridge Railway disappears on the extreme right. *Robert Anderson*

SHORT MEMORIES

24.4.62: A2/3 Pacific 60516 *Hycilla* works the 8.15am Newcastle-Cardiff to Derby.

31.3.62: A4s 60015 and 60021, A3 60039 and Type 3 D6707 arrive at Victoria with Tottenham fans for an FA Cup semi-final at Hillsborough.

14.7.62: Darnall Jubilee No. 45656 *Cochrane* noted at Scarborough with special 1X53 from Birmingham.

12.3.64: WR 4-6-0 7912 *Little Linford Hall* reaches Victoria deputising for a failed diesel.

15.8.64: WR 4-6-0 6858 *Woolston Grange* is at Victoria with the 8.55am Bournemouth-Leeds and works on to Huddersfield.

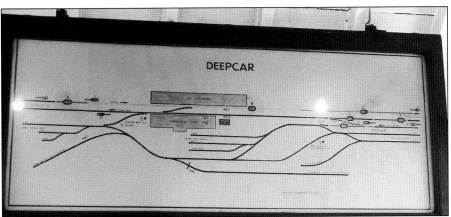

Above: The signalman at Deepcar calls forward the Class 20 which is crossing over after bringing a trip freight for the Stocksbridge Railway. It is June 1985. Deepcar station closed to passengers on 15th June 1959. It was listed in 1956 as having a 5-ton crane and being equipped to handle general goods and livestock. At the time of this picture it still received incoming coal.

Centre: The signalbox diagramme, showing the Stocksbridge Railway connection on the left and the coal merchant's siding immediately behind the station buildings.

Bottom: The Deepcar pilot, No. 08335, brings new 51 tonne scrap carriers across the station approach road while en-route from the Stocksbridge Railway. The coal depot is on the right. The redundant overhead line support shows that the line was electrified. *All Malcolm Roughley/Stephen Chapman archive*

Right: Although the Stocksbridge Railway had its own dedicated locomotives, since the 1970s it has more usually been worked by locomotives from the steelworks. Steelworks 0-6-0 diesel electric No. 30, built by the Yorkshire Engine Co. at Meadow Hall in 1959, works No. 2750, has a motley array of internal wagons at Ellencliffe Loop on Friday 18th December 1987 when the works was part of United Engineering Steels Ltd. In 2012 No. 30 was still active at the Stocksbridge works which is now part of Tata Steel Europe. *Adrian Booth*

Centre: Seen at Stocksbridge works on Saturday 5th September 1970 is Yorkshire Engine Co. 0-6-0 diesel electric No. 2608, built in 1956, a dedicated Stocksbridge Railway loco. Since then, only one loco has been retained for the Stocksbridge Railway and in 2012 it was steel works loco No. 38 (Yorkshire Engine Co. 2798 of 1961,) renamed *Stocksbridge Railway Co. 38.*
Adrian Booth

Left: Darnall 04/1 - original GC 2-8-0 introduced in 1911 - No. 63574 clanks down grade past Wharncliffe Wood with an express passenger on Thursday 26th August 1954. Whether this was a summer extra or a normal service, or whether 63574 had worked through from Manchester is not clear, but there were only four weeks to go to the new Woodhead Tunnel opening and the line being fully electrified. *P. J. Hughes/ Neville Stead collection*

Above: Although closed to regular services in June 1959, Wadsley Bridge station was retained for use by excursions, mainly football specials to nearby Hillsborough. *Colour-Rail*
It can be seen in this view of Class 76 No. E26057 *Ulysses,* passing on a Manchester-Sheffield service in November 1969, that the station was still maintained to public standards.
In 1988 the Football Trust and the government spent £28000 on refurbishing the station and demolishing the buildings. A run-round loop was kept when the line was singled but with the decline of football specials the station became disused.

Above: Steam still worked in Sheffield into the 1970s - at Neepsend power station where this Sentinel vertical-boilered loco, works No. 9370, built 1947, worked alongside a diesel built by Thomas Hill of Kilnhurst. This view is dated 28th September 1972 but the Sentinel had gone within a couple more years and the power station closed not long after.

Right: This westbound freight hauled by 76003 on Wednesday 11th July 1979 is about to pass Neepsend power station. This view amply illustrates the terrain which westbound trains had to surmount.
Both Adrian Booth

Above: Ex-Great Central "Sir Sam Fay" 4-6-0, LNER Class B2 No. 5428 *City of Liverpool* takes water on the turntable road at Neepsend engine shed on Sunday 2nd July 1939. The engine and the kilns of the Sheffield Brick Co.'s works behind it have a solid, indistructable look but, of course, both are long gone. *Neville Stead collection*

Established by the Manchester, Sheffield & Lincolnshire Railway, Neepsend was the main - and only - Great Central motive power depot for Sheffield providing everything from express passenger engines to goods engines and shunting pilots - a role for which it became hopelessly inadequate as the railway grew. In 1935 the cramped site and its congested six-road straight shed was having to cope with an allocation of 96 locomotives. A comparison with Darnall, its 10-road steam shed and extensive facilities shows the huge gulf between Neepsend and what was needed. Following the move to Darnall in 1943, Neepsend was converted into a carriage and wagon repair shop in which role it survived until the 1960s. The shed, which had a twin pitched roof, was demolished in 1969 and the site of engine shed and brickworks is now occupied by the Parkwood Industrial Estate.

Below: The layout at Neepsend engine shed as it was in 1935. Besides the 59ft 10in turntable, inside the shed building was a repair shop on the north side connected to three roads by a traverser. Upon conversion to a carriage and wagon shop, the turntable was removed but the siding to the brickworks remained. By the 1950s, the sidings into the council yard had also been removed. *Not to scale*

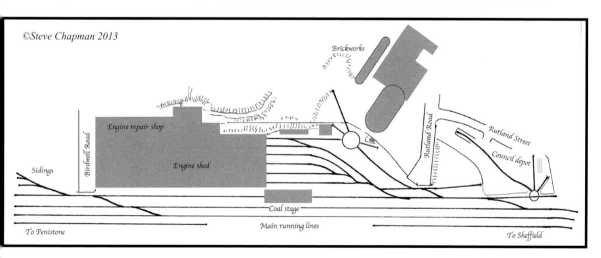

Batchelors Sidings, Wadsley Bridge: The 1969 Eastern Region Sectional Appendix stated that drivers of movements requiring to return from these sidings "in the wrong direction to the signal box in the rear" are authorised to do so on the authority of the signalman without a Wrong Line Order form. In this case, this meant over the Down Main between Oughty Bridge and Wadsley Bridge. The connection with the sidings was operated by a ground frame electrically controlled from Wadsley Bridge signal box.

Above: Class B5 4-6-0 No. 5182 is among engines having to be stabled in the overspill sidings west of Neepsend shed, beyond Birdwell Road, in this pre-1946 scene. No. 5182 is from a class introduced by the Great Central in 1902 to the design of J. G. Robinson. The GC 4-6-0s were rapidly withdrawn during the 1940s, replaced by the new B1s, and but for B4 No. 61482 *Immingham*, all had gone by 1950. *N. E. Stead colln.*

Below: Viewed from Sheffield No. 2 signal box on a miserable wet day some time after 1946, LNER C13 4-4-2T No. 7406 rushes past Bridgehouses goods station with a class B stopping train to Penistone. The points it is passing over form the junction with the Spital Tunnel incline down to Wicker, the entrance to which is beyond the wagons on the left. The main goods warehouse is the long shed immediately on the right with the tranship shed on the extreme right. *Tom Greaves*

Alan Ashley began his railway service in May 1949 as a junior clerk in the yardmaster's office at Bridgehouses.

"It was a good job for an enthusiast. I spent a third of my time in the office, a third on the footplate of the N5 shunter and a third in No.2 signal box.

"Going to work I'd get off the bus in Effingham Street, then up in the goods lift - totally unauthorized, into the telegraph office to collect the mail then walk over the Wicker Viaduct and up the line to Bridgehouses. I lived at Dinnington and when I qualified for a pass I started going to work on the train from Kiveton Park, just as the B1s were replacing the Directors and Atlantics. I remember a wooden station at Waleswood Junction where a curve went down to Killamarsh which was used mainly by coal and fish trains.

"I dealt with the yard sheets which the shunters had to fill in from Bernard Road and Bridgehouses with all trains, the engine numbers and I suppose someone could see from it how the yards performed.

"We handled all perishables at Bridgehouses and it was a job for the shunter to get right. The N4 was there three shifts apart from going for coal and water. We had an inspector at Bridgehouses and Bernard Road while the other yards had head shunters or foremen. We had guards which we also supplied in the summer for excursions to seaside resorts such as Scarborough and Blackpool.

"We were involved with local trips, shifting traffic to Bernard Road and back, and to the coal drops at Neepsend. All the shunting at Bridgehouses was done from the west end.

"I used to have to go looking for lost wagons. I'd walk through the tunnel down to Wicker - the track was still there then. Wicker was the biggest goods yard in the whole area with two pilots.

"I got in with the Darnall men and landed a footplate ride to Leicester on a B1 with the South Yorkshireman at 80mph through Loughborough, and from Victoria to Manchester through the Woodhead Tunnel. There the driver told me to put a handkerchief over my face and sit on the floor."

Upon completing two years national service in 1953, Alan went to work in the Midland lines Sheffield control office which was situated opposite Rotherham Westgate station - as "wagon waller."

"This was a class 5 assistant controller. It was all wagon statistics and not much impact on operating."

From 1959 to 1961 he was Sheffield Board controller covering Wincobank to Totley Tunnel East.

"There were four boards with a controller and assistant on each who talked to the signal boxes. The others were the Staveley Board which included the Old Road and Bradway to Horns Bridge, the Masborough Board covering Renishaw to Wath Road, and a board for Wath Road-Normanton.

"One of the main jobs was provision of motive power for the "hot dogs" - movements of hot steel between the various steel works before it cooled off too much. Frequently I had to take engines off whatever they were doing at the time in order to move a "hot dog." They nearly always involved using the main line.

"Occasionally a driver reported a fault on a loco and we had to consider whether to keep the train in Midland station and await a replacement from Millhouses or to change the engines at Millhouses. There were four tracks then so we didn't block anything but it wasn't a popular move.

"The loco sidings and turntable at Midland were still in use then for the odd engine - engines off the Leeds trains were usually turned there.

"One night I didn't get the best of write-ups. I had a report of a bump on the line at Grimesthorpe with a passenger train still to come, so I got the yard inspector at Grimesthorpe, Ernest Dodson, to walk the line with a handlamp looking for a problem. I'd told the signalman at Brightside to let the train leave Brightside station and proceed to the next signal box at Upwell Street - and it sat there for 45 minutes with the inspector looking for a non-existent bump on the line.

"In 1948 I got a ride round the goods curve from Wincobank North to West - the only time. It was on a football special from Rotherham to Tranmere.

"The big event of the night was the Condor with the Metrovicks on and everyone was on tenterhooks as to whether it would make it through our patch. I don't remember it failing while I was on duty but there was talk in Control that it had failed. It went via the Old Road so it didn't come through the Sheffield Board.

"The big event of the day was the Thames-Clyde Express. It was the premier train yet there were no special measures for it, such as double block signalling, but you made sure you made no silly requirements when those trains were about.

Bridgehouses goods yard looking east in about 1951 with the tranship shed on the left. *Alan Ashley*
The 1956 Handbook of Stations listed Bridgehouses as having a maximum crane capacity of 50 tons and equipped to deal with all classes of goods except coal, minerals and livestock. Beside the main two-road warehouse, two-road tranship shed and one-road grain warehouse, the site included a one-road potato warehouse and a two-road open sided shed plus support buildings.

Left: N4 0-6-2Ts were the usual yard pilots at Bridgehouses. N4 No. 69229 stands alongside the goods offices on Saturday 4th November 1950.
Alan Ashley

Bottom: In about 1950, ex-Railway Operating Division O4/3 2-8-0 No. 63859 hauls a class K mineral train past the divergence of the Spital Tunnel branch, the cess of which is just visible in the bottom left hand corner. More clearly visible on the left is the cattle dock which nestled in the fork of the junction.
Alan Ashley

Bridgehouses Goods booked arrivals and departures 17th June-8th September 1963

am

12.10	9T17	11.59pm from Bernard Road
12.30MX	5M10	to Guide Bridge
12.40MX	5M11	to Liverpool Brunswick
1.0MX	8T17	to Bernard Road
1.36MX		Light electric engine conveying train crews to Victoria
2.0-2.10MX	6E27	8.45pm Huskisson-Bernard Road
4.42MX	4E80	2.30am from Dringhouses
4.43MO	7E76	3.15am from Dewsnap
5.0MX		Class 8 to Barnsley Jn.
5.10MX	4E31	10.10pm from St. Pancras
5.42MX	5E22	4.15am from Dewsnap
5.50MX	8T17	5.40am from Bernard Road
6.23	5E76	1.10am from Woodford
6.25	8T17	to Bernard Road
6.30-45SO	8M90	6.25am Bernard Road-Mottram
8.8SO	8T03	to Oughty Bridge
8.10	8T17	8am from Bernard Road

pm

12.30	8T17	to Bernard Road
4.5	8T17	to Bernard Road
10.0-20	7M46	9.55pm Bernard Road-Mottram
10.25SX	7T13	9.15pm from Engine Shed Sidings
11.21SX		Class 5 9.5pm from Doncaster Belmont

Above: In this view taken from the cattle dock in the previous picture, B1 4-6-0 No. 61156 passes the Bridgehouses grain warehouse as she sets out from Victoria station with the Harwich-Liverpool boat train. No. 69227 is the N4 waiting at the signal. *Alan Ashley*

Below: When the B1s entered service in the 1940s, they quickly became standard motive power for passenger services of all classes on the non-electrified GC lines from Sheffield. Resplendent in LNER apple green livery, practically new 1158 enters Victoria station from the west at the head of an Up express. Towering above, behind the signals, is Wigfalls flour mill. *Tom Greaves*

LONDON & NORTH EASTERN RAILWAY CO.

DISTRICT PASSENGER AGENT'S OFFICE,

VICTORIA STATION,

SHEFFIELD.

PRESENTED BY...

Above: The variety of motive power to be savoured at Victoria in the 1950s was no less enthralling than at Midland. A5 4-6-2T No. 69806 from Colwick shed, backs through the station after coming off an arriving local passenger train, probably from Nottingham.
Tom Greaves

Right: Before departing with the 9.47am to Manchester, driver Fred Tyler and fireman Brian Woodhead pose with V2 No. 60890 for the camera of Doncaster Works premium apprentice Tom Greaves, who was at the time gaining experience in a placement at Darnall.

As recounted by Tom in Railway Memories No. 26, driver Tyler was fed up with the dangerous antics of wiring gangs installing the overhead wires as they routinely ignored engine whistles. It was on this run that he encountered a wireman at Dunford Bridge slinging connectors with his feet on the anchor wire and hanging onto the suspension wires. As per the norm, Fred's whistle was ignored. "I'll shift the ***," said Fred and with that he dropped the reverser down the scale which resulted in a vertical blast of exhaust. They had never seen a wireman move so fast.

Left: EM2 No. 27002 *Aurora* was a strange looking beast which appeared to be wearing spectacles. The rotating lenses were designed to stop the windscreen icing up during winter journeys over the wilds of Woodhead - a method adopted from North Sea trawlers.
She is seen at Victoria on 15th June 1963.
Peter Cookson

Above: The tall chimney stacks of the Royal Victoria Hotel (built 1862 and sold off by BR in 1982) loom large on the right as B1 No. 1279 waits at the west end of platform 2. The view is from the horse and carriage dock.
Tom Greaves

GC 4-6-0s soon to retire. Centre: B7/1 LNER No. 1370 stands at the east end of platform 4 while one of her successors, B1 No. 1212, is in platform 5. The B7s were of a Robinson design introduced in 1921. *N. E. Stead colln.*

Bottom: With 6ft 9in driving wheels well evident, No. 61497 at patform 5 on 26th October 1948, is Class B3/3, a B3/2 rebuilt after fracturing a cylinder in 1943 with a B1 boiler and two cylinders. The B3/2 was a Gresley rebuild of the original 4-cylinder B3/1 introduced in 1918. Despite her youth, 61497 was withdrawn in February 1949. *P.J. Hughes/N.E.Stead colln.*

Bellcode publisher Stephen Chapman's first memory of Sheffield's railways was in summer 1959: "It was the first Saturday in August and we were being met by an uncle at Rugby Central. I had an embryonic interest in railways and had read about Sheffield Victoria's new 'ultra-modern' buffet. On arrival from York, my parents retired to the new buffet while I stood outside on platfiorm 4 watching the comings and goings, excited at seeing electric trains for the first time. Eventually the dark shape of an electric loco far away at the west end got nearer and our Rugby train arrived. How disappointed I was that our electric was taken off and replaced by a run-of-the-mill B1. I calculate that our train was probably the 2.10pm Manchester-Marylebone. For a time this 8 year-old stood by the open droplight in the door behind the engine as we passed a long line of brand new or freshly painted 16-ton mineral wagons shortly after setting off. I was on the wrong side to see Darnall shed. How little I knew then.

"In 1972 I looked like having an enforced stay in Sheffield. It was Saturday 13th May when a friend and I were returning to York from an open day at Toton. It was during an industry-wide work to rule which involved the newly-established Industrial Relations Court and a BRB directive that no trains would run on Sunday, all terminating at 22.00 at the most covenient point.

"Eventually making our way back to Sheffield via Derby at 19.15hrs on a train running two hours late, we awaited the 19.37 Newcastle due at 20.15. My friend had a transistor radio and before long we were joined by railwaymen listening for the Industrial Relations Court ruling. It was that all staff must work normally from Monday pending further negotiations. Not much use to us at the time. As we stood there, the station announcer continually proclaimed: "There will be no more trains to.... tonight." First Hull, and a Hull driver with us felt the cold realisation that his last homeward working was cancelled. Then came Derby, Birmingham, New Mills, Lincoln and Leeds. By the time our Newcastle train came, it was the last surviving departure from Sheffield. But with "Peak" No. 43 raring to go at 20.40, there was no relief crew to take it forward. A Sheffield driver and second man agreed to work it so long as a taxi was arranged to bring them back, and a York guard needing to get home offered his

services. We had a full crew but as precious minutes ticked by, the signal stayed red. The Masborough signalman had signed off and the York line was shut. All hope seemed lost but then an announcement advised Leeds passengers to catch our train and change at Wakefield - what did that mean? The Barnsley line was still open but our guard didn't know the road. Luckily, a Leeds guard otherwise unable to get home acted as conductor. We felt a warm feeling as the train creaked round the sharp curve from Wincobank and up to Chapeltown. A classic example of railway staff pulling together in a crisis - even when in dispute.

"Sunday 21st January 1973 provided another memorable Sheffield experience. This was the weekend when the power box was commissioned requiring the closure of Midland station and temporary reopening of Victoria - an occasion not to be missed. Our diverted DMU from Doncaster to Victoria took us via Masborough, Treeton North and Tinsley Yard. It was a foul wet day and the rain was turning to snow; the windows were so steamed up we struggled to see much. After Broughton Lane, we noticed a grimy saddletank which I later found was at Brown Bayley's works. Victoria presented a depressing sight. DMUs idled impatiently, their blue exhaust mingling with the rain cascading through the holes in the platform canopies.

"We then headed off in a DMU over Woodhead to Manchester. As we climbed steadly up the gradient to Penistone the snow got heavier and by Dunford Bridge it was up to rail level.

"In the following four years I visited the Sheffield area as a member of the Chief Civil Engineer's inspection team - alas always a little disappointing as nearly all Sheffield inspections were conducted by road. At Wharncliffe Wood on another very wet day what struck me was the smell of electrical burning as the rain lashed down on the overhead wires.

"My final Woodhead trip came on 19th August 1980 when in the line of duty I accompanied P.W.B. Semmens in the cab of 76003 at the head of a Rotherwood-Garston coal train. He was doing a Practice and Performance article for Railway Magazine. The drivers generally referred to the 76s simply as the "Bo-Bos" and they called the EMUs on the Glossop and Hadfield suburban services "Clockwork mice."

The view from platform 4 in LNER days with ex-Great Central B7/2 4-6-0 No. 5484 on an Up express prior to the 1946 renumbering
Tom Greaves

Above: The Flying Scotsman has always been an indisputable symbol of the East Coast main line yet in the early 1950s she was a Leicester engine working expresses on the GC main line, a time when the GC could boast motive power to match any main line. Wearing her 38C shedplate, No. 60103 waits to leave Victoria with a Marylebone express. *A. L. Brown/Neville Stead collection*

Below: The world-famous A3, preserved as LNER No. 4472, makes a return visit to the same spot with a 1960s railtour. These engines graced the GC as early as 1924 when as A1s newly built at Doncaster they were run-in on the route. *Neville Stead collection*

Above: Besides all the glamourous express passenger engines, goods engines were constantly dragging long processions of rumbling wagons through Victoria station. Doncaster-based Class 02/3 2-8-0 No. 63978 reminds us of the ever-present Great Northern influence as it heads east with a class K train of empties. No. 63978 was one of a batch introduced in 1932 with side window cabs - much needed for winter runs over Woodhead. Much work to increase capacity at Victoria station took place in the early 20th century when the station was expanded with an extra platform and the running lines to Woodburn Junction were quadrupled. *Tom Greaves*

Below: During steam days the Harwich-Liverpool boat train could usually be relied upon to bring exotic motive power to Sheffield Victoria. This was the return working leaving for Harwich on Thursday 25th August 1932 when original Great Eastern B12 4-6-0 No. 8568, fitted with a feedwater heater, was in charge. *Neville Stead collection*

Above: Another of the mineral trains trundling through Victoria is hauled eastwards along the Up Goods line by Darnall's Class 04/3 2-8-0 No. 63783. The 04/3s were a variant of the original Robinson GC 1911 design introduced during the first world war for the army's Railway Operating Division and taken into LNER stock from 1924. 'Modernist' screens have been installed to shelter passengers on platform 5 from the North wind that would sweep across this elevated position. *Tom Greaves*

Below: BR Standard Class 7 Pacific No. 70000 *Britannia*, then of Stratford shed, starts the return to Harwich in September 1958 after taking over the boat train from an electric loco. This engine is still with us but the chances of seeing her at this spot again must be minimal. In 2012 all that remained of Victoria station was one disused overgrown platform and a single track. *Neville Stead collection*

Passenger trains when conveying four-wheeled vehicles of less than 15 feet wheelbase in any position on the train, must not exceed 40mph on the Up and Down lines between Manchester and Sheffield. The restriction must also be applied to "LNER" horse boxes with a 14 feet wheelbase which are lettered "May run at speeds exceeding 60mph on LNER only."
BR Eastern Region Sectional Appendix 1969

Above: With Sheffield No. 4 signal box behind it, an unidentified J11 0-6-0 provides rear end assistance to a westbound freight approaching Victoria station in the early 1950s. *Tom Greaves*

Below: Coming into the station past No. 4 box, D11/1 4-4-0 No. 62663 *Prince Albert* arrives with a class B passenger service. Although the new B1s quickly replaced the older GC passenger locos in the 1940s, the "Large Director" D11s survived. In BR days most (the D11/2s) were in Scotland but the eleven D11/1s were allocated mainly to Immingham, Lincoln, Northwich or Trafford Park. When displaced by diesels, they were transferred to Darnall and retained to provide additional power during the busy summer service right up to 1960. The picture is undated but must be between 1958 and 1960 as an N5 0-6-2T is on Pullman cars in the right distance. The signal box lasted until 1986 when it was abolished upon closure of Nunnery carriage sidings. *Neville Stead collection*

Above: Electrification is coming and signalling modernisation is under way but it won't affect this train which will remain steam throughout until its withdrawal in 1960. B1 4-6-0 No. 61182 starts the complete set of crimson and cream coaches forming the South Yorkshireman on its way to Marylebone after taking over from the Low Moor engine, in all probability a Stanier Class 5, which has brought it from Bradford. During the 1950s, the Low Moor Class 5 would then work the York-Bournemouth to Leicester and return with the northbound working before taking over the returning South Yorkshireman. *Neville Stead collection*

Below: Victoria saw some rare visitors in its time but this must be the rarest. Southern Railway West Country class Pacific No. 34006 *Bude* departs with an Up express on Wednesday 9th June 1948 during the 1948 locomotive exchanges. This was when newly-formed BR conducted a series of trials to assess the performance of locomotives from the Big Four companies on routes other than their own, the results then being incorporated in a new standard design for the whole network. The first coach is the dynamometer car assigned to record *Bude's* performance. *Neville Stead collection*

Above: Leicester V2 No. 60863 makes a determined start from Victoria with the up Master Cutler some time before 1958 when it became a diesel-hauled Pullman. *Tom Greaves*

Left: The scene at Victoria on Sunday 21st January 1973 when it was temporarily reopened during the commissioning of Sheffield power signal box.

Below: A last sad look at Victoria from the cab of 76003 on a Rotherwood-Garston coal train on Tuesday 19th August 1980. Demolition detritus lines the platforms.
Both Stephen Chapman

Right: N5 0-6-2T No. 69295 shunts at the entrance to Park Goods, alongside the eastern exit from Victoria station in about 1956. On the left can be seen Blast Lane depot. *Tom Greaves*

Park was listed in the 1956 Handbook of Stations as being equipped to handle general goods only with no permanent crane. Blast Lane, described as a public depot, was listed as having a 10-ton crane capacity and equipped for general goods only.

Below: With Park goods yard in the left distance, B17/6 4-6-0 No. 61619 *Welbeck Abbey* - one of those rebuilt from 1947 with a B1 boiler - storms away with the boat train to Harwich. *Tom Greaves*

The B17s took over many GC main line express workings from GC Atlantics, 4-6-0s and Director 4-4-0s in the 1930s but from 1938 heavier loadings saw A1 Pacifics and V2s diagrammed for much of their work. GE section-based B17s continued to work the boat train until replaced by Britannia Pacifics in the late 1950s.

Above: Seen from Sheffield No. 5 signal box, *Flying Scotsman* is departing Victoria with another 1960s Great Central railtour. The signals in the background denote Nunnery cutting and the line into Midland station. *Tom Greaves*

Below: The going-away shot of the previous picture reveals the expanse of Nunnery carriage sidings up ahead and a great old British name in tools on the right. No. 5 box would be abolished under the 1960s modernisation. *Tom Greaves*

Above: Also seen from No. 5 box, a B1 and bike with vans in the carriage sidings east of Victoria station. *Tom Greaves*

Right: An automated coal depot was established at Nunnery by British Fuel Co. and, railway-wise, even that had closed by 1982. *Maria*, the resident Ruston & Hornsby 0-4-0 diesel electric (works No. 384144 of 1955)is pictured here. Sheffield Parkway is on the left. *Adrian Booth*

Below: The view from Nunnery carriage sidings as a K2 2-6-0 on a westbound goods blows off impatiently while held at a signal. The tank wagon bears the initials of the Cheshire Lines Committee of which both the Midland and GC were partners along with the GN. On the left a cleaner gets to grips with Manchester coaching set No. 18. A chimney in the centre background sports Wedgewood-style decoration. *Tom Greaves*

Above: On the GC Rotherham line at Broughton Lane on a misty late 1963 morning, B1 No. 61121 heads towards Woodburn Junction with a very precious load. Behind it is the world's fastest steam locomotive, LNER A4 Pacific No. 4468 *Mallard*, on its way to the transport museum at Clapham following restoration at Doncaster Works. On the left are Broughton Lane sidings and goods yard with its modern goods shed, rebuilt in the late 1950s. The 1956 Handbook of Stations listed Broughton Lane as having a 20-ton crane capacity and equipped to handle general goods. The passenger station here closed on 3rd April 1956 but the goods yard outlived the 1960s. *Tom Greaves*

Below: The same spot on 22nd May 1981 with EM1 No. 76054, formerly *Pluto*, coming from Tinsley Yard on a train of 16-ton mineral wagons, some of which appear to be loaded with scrap. The goods yard and sidings are still in business on the left, the only major changes being electrification and abandonment of the siding on the right.

In steam days, banking engines were provided to assist heavy freights over this steep and curving stretch where the gradient peaks at 1 in 70. *Adrian Booth*

am		pm	
4.27MX	Class 7 10.25pm from Whitemoor *Assured Arrival*	1.14	8T08 12.40pm from Woodhouse
4.59-5.27MX	8T14 4.40am Bernard Road-Rotherham Central	1.43	Class 8 12.20pm from Worksop
	Assured Arrival	2.4-2.52	8T01 Bernard Road-Rotherham Road
5.44MX	Class 8 4.45am from Worksop	2.30	8T09 to Masborough Sorting Sidings
6.5-7.5MX	Class 8 4.40am Warsop Jn.-Aldwarke Main Colliery	2.40	8T15 to Chapeltown Central
6.15	8T10 to Tinsley West Jn. *To work as req'd by Control*	3.31	Class 8 2.40pm from Staveley Central
6.19-6.47MO	8T14 6am Bernard Road-Rotherham Central	3.36MX	Class 8 3.5am from Ickles Sidings
7.25	Class 8 to Wath Yard	5.45	7T13 to Wincobank Sidings
7.35	8T09 to Rotherham Road	5.49	Class 8 5.30pm from Bernard Road
8.0	8T11 to Meadow Hall	6.35	8T01 to Ickles Sidings
8.6-8.35MO	Class 8 6.30am Warsop Jn.-Aldwarke Main Colliery	6.50	Class 8 4.45pm from Barrow Hill
8.12-8.20MX	Class 8 7.5am Seymour Jn.-Rotherham Road	7.1	Class 8 6.10pm from Staveley Central
8.13	8T25 to Attercliffe Yard	9.26	Class 8 8.15pm from Worksop
11.53	8T25 to Firth's Sidings	10.30	8T60 to Wath Yard
	Light engine movements not shown	11.10-30	8E31 8.40pm Annesley-Ickles Sidings

Tinsley East Junction-Woodburn Junction was shown in the Eastern Region 1969 Sectional Appendix as signalled by Track Circuit Block with signal boxes at Tinsley East Jn.(1353yds from Ickles,) Shepcote Lane (355yds,) and Woodburn Junction(2 miles 389yds.)

Additional running lines were Down Goods Tinsley East-Shepcote Lane, and Shepcote Lane signals 12-17, and Up Goods Shepcote Lane signals 25-28. They were signalled by Track Circuit Block Permissive. The Down direction was towards Woodburn Junction. The gradient was rising from 1 in 96 to 1 in 70/72.

SHORT MEMORIES

Summer 1964: T.W.Ward's at Broughton Lane cutting up WR Castle and County 4-6-0s, 28xx 2-8-0s, 43xx 2-6-0s and SR S15 4-6-0s.

3.9.66: Brush 4 No. D1572 brings the last Bournemouth-Newcastle via the GC into Victoria.

4.1.69: "Peaks" Nos. 15 and 53 are on football specials from Leeds to Wadsley bridge

Among the many private sidings connected to the Woodburn Junction-Tinsley Junction section was T. W. Ward's scrap works at Tinsley. This view, looking south with the GC line out of the picture on the left, shows Fowler 0-4-0 diesel hydraulic 22975 of 1942 at work there on Saturday 3rd April 1976. *Adrian Booth*

Left: Tinsley Junction in the early 1960s with York V2 No. 60828 heading the York-Bournemouth formed of Southern Region green stock. In 2013 only a single line remains here while Supertram tracks run alongside on the left, curving round to Meadow Hall Interchange and the giant shopping centre which replaced the works buildings on the left.
Tom Greaves

Below: English Electric Type 4 No. 40196 leads a mixed unfitted freight round from Tinsley Junction and over the River Don to Tinsley East Junction on Friday 31st December 1976. The Sheffield Road overbridge in the background marks the site of Tinsley station and the start of the north curve into Tinsley Yard.
Adrian Booth

Ecclesfield East-Shepcote Lane was listed in the Eastern Region 1969 Sectional Appendix as double track and signalled by Absolute Block. Signal boxes were at Ecclesfield East, Grange Lane(1311yds from Ecclesfield,) Meadow Hall(1m 512yds,) Tinsley West Junction(927yds) and Shepcote Lane(1 mile 91yds.) Up and Down refuge sidings were provided at Grange Lane. The maximum speed was 30mph. Direction of travel was Up from Tinsley. The rising gradient between Grange Lane and Ecclesfield East was 1 in 67 and rear banking assistance could at times be needed, the instruction given that the assisting locomotive must not be coupled to the train.

Above: Beneath the M1 Tinsley Viaduct, Type 1s Nos. 20127 and 20061 head a train of empty 21-ton hoppers for Smithywood coking plant over Tinsley West Junction on 20th March 1976. The train is coming from Tinsley Junction and joining the curve from Tinsley East. According to the headcode discs, the train is a class 7. The signal box closed with the branch in July 1987 and trams now follow this route en-route to Meadow Hall Interchange.

Centre: Until 1990 the Blackburn Meadows sewerage works had an extensive internal railway. Two year-old Thomas Hill 4-wheel diesel hydraulic 265v is seen there on 11th February 1978. *Both Adrian Booth* By this time strictly internal, the skip wagons once had plates reading: "City of Sheffield sewage disposal department. Return empty to Tinsley Siding" and "To run between Ickles Sidings and Thrybergh Tip."

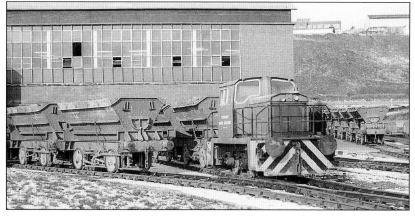

Bottom: Sidings which once formed part of the Wincobank-Meadow Hall spur, occupied on 30th September 1999 by the collection of the South Yorkshire Railway Preservation Society which aimed to preserve the Chapeltown branch. Wincobank gas works is on the left. *Stephen Chapman*

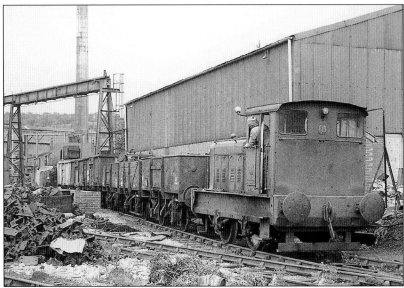

TOP: After the Yorkshire Engine Company went out of business in 1965, its Meadow Hall works site was occupied by McCall's steel company. During its 100-year history, the Yorkshire Engine Co. built nearly 3000 locomotives, its later speciality being, appropriately, diesel shunters for the steel industry, many of which remain in service in 2013. Diesel hydraulic 0-6-0 works No. 2896, built 1964 - an unsold new loco acquired with the Yorkshire Engine Co. site - shunts what was by then British Steel McCalls on Friday 22nd April 1977.

CENTRE: Among the various private sidings connected to the Blackburn Valley line was Roe Brothers iron and steel merchants. They had 1962-built Ruston & Hornsby 88DS class 4-wheel diesel *Elizabeth*(works No. 466630 of 1962) which is seen shunting a selection of BR open wagons on Friday 1st July 1977.

BELOW: Type 1s Nos. 20025 and 20130 negotiate the level crossing at Grange Lane with a coke train from Smithywood on Tuesday 29th May 1979. *All Adrian Booth*

Meadow Hall and Grange Lane stations closed to passengers on 7th December 1953. The former closed to goods on 12th July 1965, and the latter on 31st December 1956, both retaining private siding trafiic. In summer 1963, the line was used by 15 Up and 14 Down freights. These included 8 reversing at Meadow Hall for transfer with the Midland lines, plus the 7.25am Broughton Lane-Wath and 8.30am Wath-Ickles class 8s, the only trains travelling the line's full length.

V2 2-6-2 No. 60821, a visitor from Peterborough's New England depot, rests at the east end of Darnall shed in the early 1960s. Behind it, inside, is Midland 1F 0-6-0T No. 41875 from Canklow. *Tom Greaves*

Opened in 1943 to replace Neepsend, Darnall motive power depot was coded 39B by BR's Eastern Region(Gorton was 39A) and, as with all the region's GC lines, was part of the Great Northern lines motive power management unit. In 1955 Darnall became top shed of a separate Sheffield District and was coded 41A.

Facilities included a 10-road "West Light" running shed, two-road repair shop with wheel drop and hoist, mechanical coaling plant, 200ft wet ash pit, 100,000 gallon water tank and 70ft turntable. A four-road electric locomotive shed added in 1952 was adapted as a diesel depot when electric locomotive maintenance was concentrated on Manchester's Reddish depot under the 1958 reorganisation.

When Tinsley diesel depot opened in April 1964 all maintenance work was transferred there and Tinsley assumed the 41A shedcode, Darnall becoming the subordinate 41B. Darnall's main line diesel allocation and about half its shunters were transferred to Tinsley; its surviving steam allocation having already been withdrawn or transferred to remaining steam sheds, mainly Canklow, Langwith Junction or sheds in the Doncaster Division. Darnall continued with an allocation of 350hp(Class 08) shunters which stood at 43 in May 1965, but t closed altogether on 4th October when those shunters were mostly transferred to Tinsley with a few dispersed to other depots. Even then Darnall continued as a servicing and stabling point for diesel multiple units operating around Sheffield (receiving the TOPs depot code of DA) and, roofless, as a carriage and wagon repair shop until the late 1980s. Some of its last work included stripping withdrawn DMU cars prior to scrapping. The shed was demolished in 1994 and the site redeveloped with modern warehouses and business units.

Locomotives allocated to 39B Sheffield September 1950: B1 4-6-0: 61145/50/1/2/3/4/69/79/81/3/311/2/3/4/5/6/7/27; O4 2-8-0: 63574/81/3/604/5/9/22/9/61/75/80/5/710/4/33/4/7/66/71/83/90//7/821/2/46/50/60/82/8/91; J11 0-6-0: 64291/336/60/73/82/412/9/41/3/5/7; J39 0-6-0: 64746/53/808/9/78/87/912/9/41/3/5/73; C13 2-4-2T: 67404/6; Y3 4wVBT: 68176/84; J50 0-6-0T: 68928/83/90; J72 0-6-0T: 69015; N4 0-6-2T: 69225/7/8/9/30/1/2/3/4/5/6/9/40/2/4/5/6. Total: 94

Locomotives allocated to 41A Sheffield Darnall July 1962: 7P 4-6-0: 45536; 6P 4-6-0: 45570/6/94/656/83/725; 7P 4-6-0: 46151/64; B1 4-6-0: 61004/27/33/44/7/50/1/6/90/4/1104/5/9/11/2/38/9/50/1/2/3/4/5/64/6/9/81/228/34/49/66/312/3/5/27/34/72/8/99; O4 2-8-0: 63574/604/9/21/4/45/58/85/95/734/7/42/83/821/2/46/50/2/81/2; J11 0-6-0: 64329/73/94/419/45; 350hp 0-6-0: D3086/127/9/31/251/2/3/4/88/9/93/325/6/30/6/476/574/5/659/60/1/2/3/4/85/98/701/2/3/7/27/4028-74/89/90/1/2/3/4; Brush Type 2: D5655/6/7/84/5/6/7/8/9/90/1/2/3/805-34/36-51; Brush Type 4(2000hp Type 2): D5835; English Electric Type 3: D6742/3/4/5/6/7; English Electric Type 1: D8020/1/2/ 3/4/50-69. Total: 247. Also based at Darnall was 20-ton steam breakdown crane No.105.

On 3rd March 1963, Alex Scott noted the following locomotives on Darnall shed: Rebuilt Patriot 4-6-0: 45536 *Private W. Wood VC;* Jubilee 4-6-0: 45570 *New Zealand*/45594 *Bhopal*/45656 *Cochrane;* 8F 2-8-0: 48200; B1 4-6-0: 61044/50/51/94/ 109/43/52/210/61249 *FitzHerbert Wright*/72/305/13/15/77; O4 2-8-0: 63574/609/21/4/45/58/95/737/42/64/83/821/2/36/81/ 02; WD 2-8-0: 90162/582; Brush Type 4 prototype: D0280 *Falcon;* 350hp 0-6-0: D3131/702/40/50/1/65/74/82/5/94; Brush Type 2: D5520/684/99/805/13/23/5/6/38/44/5/51; English Electric Type 3: D6745/6/7/8/9/50/4/96/802/3/6/8/10/1/2/4/58; English Electric Type 1: D8023/53/4/60/1/3. Total: 85

Above: The O4 2-8-0s always had a considerable presence at Darnall. Ex-R.O.D 04/3 No. 63821 is topped-up by the coaling plant at 1.49pm on Saturday 12th September 1959. *Robert Anderson*

Left: The view from the coaling plant with a B1? being replenished between turns on the boat train *Tom Greaves*

Darnall booked pilot duties 17th June-8th September 1963: Barnsley Jn. No.1: *Shunts Barnsley Jn., Penistone and Bullhouse, and works trips Barnsley Jn.-Penistone and Hazlehead, and Barnsley;* Barnsley Jn. No.2: *Yard pilot* Beighton: *Shunts Beighton Tip;* Broughton Lane No.1: *Marshalls as required;* Broughton Lane No.2: *Shunt and service private sidings;* Deepcar *Shunting at Deepcar, General Refractories Lowood's Sidings, Wharncliffe Wood, and Wortley Works trips to and from exchange sidings* Bridgehouses No.1: *Shunts west end of yard* Bridgehouses No.2: *Shunts east end of yard;* No 3 Parkway Yard and Parkway Market: *Shunts as required;* No. 4 Harvest Lane: *Shunts coal drop and works trips as required;* No. 6 Bernard Road West: *shunts west end of Bernard Road;* No. ? Bernard Road East: *Shunts east end of Bernard Road, also engineers' yard and ballast sidings West end 2.15-6am Sunday;* No. 9 Sheffield No. ? Down side: *shunts Sheffield No. 6 Down yard* Tinsley No. 1 and No.2: *Assisting trains as required;* Wadsley Bridge: *Shunts as required.* Three pilots were also supplied for shunting at Ickles yard and one for Rotherham Central.

Above: Darnall's repair shop must have been a vast improvement over Neepsend and, indeed, many other steam depots. C13 4-4-2T No. 67439 is seen undergoing valve and piston examination in March 1954. *Tom Greaves*

Below: The view from the east end of the depot yard with O4/2 2-8-0 No. 63682 in company with, on the right, a K3 2-6-0 and a J39 0-6-0. On the left is the light tunnel, built in the second world war so that locomotives in traffic could be examined at night during the blackout, but which after the war also proved useful as an additional inspection facility. Fluorescent strip lights illuminated the tunnel and inspection pit yet it was completely light proof. No. 63682 was originally an O4/3 but was among a batch which from 1925 had their cab and boiler mountings reduced to fit the Scottish loading gauge. *Tom Greaves*

SHORT MEMORIES

4.1.70: The last day of booked passenger services over Woodhead affected by an evening freight derailment delaying the 19.30 ex-Sheffield by 80min and causing cancellation of its return working, the last train, the 21.30 ex-Manchester. A special eventually provided to clear stranded passengers reaches Victoria at 00.45 on the 5th behind E26054 *Pluto*.

27.3.71: Wadsley Bridge receives 16 special trains for the FA Cup semi-final between Arsenal and Stoke.

W/e 13.11.72: E26050 the first loco to be renumbered under the TOPS scheme, becoming 76050.

14-28.2.72: With severely reduced traffic and power cuts due to a miners' strike, BR works the Woodhead line with diesels. Class 20 bankers needed from Sheffield or Wadsley Bridge and to pilot unbraked freights downgrade Dunford West-Woodburn Jn.

Above: One of the dwindling breed of GC Atlantics, C4 No. 2922, makes use of Darnall's 70ft vacuum-operated turntable in 1947. She is believed to have arrived with a service from Lincoln. *A. G. Ellis/Neville Stead collection*

Below: The N4 0-6-2 tanks introduced by the Manchester, Sheffield & Lincolnshire Railway in 1889 to the design of T. Parker were familiar pilots around the Sheffield GC lines. No. 69235 stands in Darnall yard while B1 No. 61314 is turned. The N4s were extinct by spring 1955 and their place taken by the slightly younger N5s. *Tom Greaves*

Facing extinction at Darnall.
Top: In the twilight of its years, GC Compound Atlantic, LNER Class C5, No. 2898 *Sir William Pollitt* **stands on Darnall shed on Sunday 10th August 1947.** *Neville Stead collection*

Below: The last ex-GC "Glenalmond" 4-6-0, Darnall's LNER Class B8 No. 1357 *Earl Roberts of Kandahar,* **about 18 months before it was withdrawn in April 1949.** *Neville Stead collection*

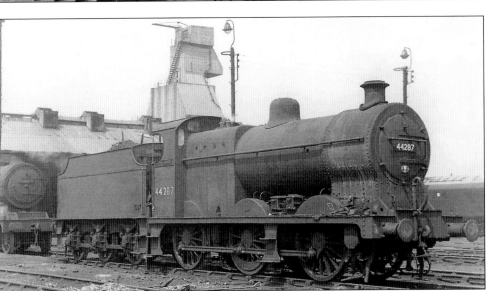

Top: One of H. A
Ivatt's Great
Northern
Atlantics, LNER
Class C1 No. 2817
towards the end of
its days when
visiting Darnall in
the late 1940s.
*Neville
Stead collection*

Centre:
Mexborough-
based WD 2-8-0
No. 90580 at the
wet ash pits in the
mid 1950s.
Tom Greaves

Bottom: Following
the closure of the
ex-Midland shed
in Sheffield
Darnall dealt with
engines from both
systems. 4F 0-6-0
No. 44287, at the
east end of the
shed, was visiting
from Barrow Hill.
Tom Greaves

Above. The J11 0-6-0s, a Robinson GC design dating from 1901, might be thought of as goods engines but in fact were mixed traffic engines, being classified 2P3F by BR. Darnall's not inconsiderable allocation could be found on local and excursion passenger duty as well as freight. No. 64441, seen on shed with B1 No. 61314, was a J11/3, a Thompson rebuild introduced in 1942 with long-travel piston valves and a higher pitched boiler. *Tom Greaves*

Left: A particularly memorable episode in Darnall's history was in 1962 when, upon closure of Millhouses, it found itself with that shed's work and a selection of ex-LMS Class 6 and 7 4-6-0s. They spent most of their time in store but Royal Scot No. 46151 *The Royal Horse Guardsman* is well oiled and has clearly seen some action.

Tom Greaves who took this photo and was traction engineer at the time recalls: "They were hardly used after being transferred to Darnall. They went to Staveley for store, then back to Darnall and were then withdrawn. As far as I recall, we got authority to put three back in service for holiday fortnight in 1962."

Top: Another of the LMS 4-6-0s which Darnall inherited from Millhouses was Rebuilt Patriot No. 45536 *Private W. Wood VC.* Around the time of this and the previous picture, Trafford Park Royal Scot No. 46158 *The Loyal Regiment* visited Darnall shed between workings.
Tom Greaves

Centre: Among ex-Great Northern K2 2-6-0s dumped in the yard on Saturday 8th October 1960 was 61761. Ex-works from Cowlairs in September 1958, some sources say it never again turned a wheel in revenue service before being scrapped at Doncaster. Others say it worked for two weeks.
Robert Anderson

Bottom: Among the D11s in winter storage on 2nd April 1960 was 62668 *Jutland.*
Robert Anderson

Above: Not forgetting that Darnall became an important diesel depot with an allocation of over 170 main line diesel locos and shunters in 1962, until superseded by Tinsley. Brush Type 2 No. D5860 stands outside the diesel shed, formerly the electric shed. New tube stock for London stands by the Cravens works on the opposite side of the main running lines. *Tom Greaves*

Below: "Built by Cravens of Sheffield" is what it says on this railcar which is clearly for export to some other land where cowcatchers are a prerequisite. Cravens was a major builder of railway rolling stock ranging from, as seen above, London tube trains to diesel multiple units for BR, as well as for export. When the firm went out of business in 1966 its rolling stock activity was acquired by Metropolitan-Cammell of Birmingham. *Tom Greaves*

Above: Class O4/8 2-8-0 No. 63645 trundles past the Cravens works with an eastbound class K goods on Saturday 23rd July 1960. This engine was one of a batch rebuilt by Thompson from 1944 onwards with a B1 boiler and side window cab.

The line from here to Woodhouse was quadrupled in the early 20th century and the 374yd Handsworth Tunnel opened out, but nowadays there are just two running lines and nothing else. A housing estate has recently been built on the Cravens works site.

Below: A stopping train from Chesterfield Central is restarted from Darnall for Handsworth(to give its full title) station's island platform by Ivatt Class 4 2-6-0 No. 43087, a Staveley Central loco, at 12.50pm on 23rd July 1960. Formerly a New England engine, 43087 has a tablet catcher for single line working on the Midland & Great Northern lines. In 2013 Darnall is the only surviving suburban station in "inner Sheffield," with an hourly Lincoln service. The goods yard stayed in business until December 1974. *Both Robert Anderson*

DAVY'S AND UNITED WORKS: Down trains conveying traffic for the above works, must detach the traffic direct into the firm's sidings from the connection in the Down Goods line at the East box, and not convey the wagons into the goods yard. *Eastern Region Sectional Appendix 1969* The Davy works rail system has been purely internal since 1982.

Left: This place is Orgreave but the nearby signal box was called Orgreaves Colliery. EM1s 76027 and 76023 are heading the Worcester Locomotive Society's Pennine Rose railtour westbound on Saturday 13th October 1979. In the background the Orgreave Colliery Railway descends to the coke and chemical plant.

Below: 76006 and 76012 pull a westbound coal train out of Rotherwood Sidings on Tuesday 7th October 1980.

Bottom: Type 1s 20035 and 20021 approach Woodhouse Junction with eastbound mineral wagons on Thursday 12th July 1979.
All Adrian Booth

Above: Looking towards Woodhouse Junction on Monday 7th July 1997. The line to Worksop and Retford goes left and that to Beighton Junction goes right. The sidings on the right were still used in 2012 by occasional coal trains reversing while running between the Old Road and the Worksop direction. The line curving immediately behind Woodhouse Junction signal box leads to disused and overgrown sidings.

Centre: Woodhouse station looking east on 7th July 1997, is of a typical MSL design which can be seen all the way to Merseyside on the Cheshire Lines. In a considerable state of disrepair, the station has since been renovated and a South Yorkshire PTE security centre occupies the rooms behind the boarded up windows on the right. *Both Stephen Chapman*

Right: The intersection bridge where the Sheffield-Retford line crosses over the Old Road, looking north on 22nd June 1977 with Type 1s 20007 and 20212 heading east. *Adrian Booth:*

Above: Withdrawn locomotives dumped in the sidings at Woodhouse Junction on Friday 3rd May 1991, including Tinsley's celebrity green-liveried "Peak" 45106. The curve to Beighton Junction is in the foreground.
Stephen Chapman

Left: Beighton station closed completely in November 1954 but the station yard still provided a connection to George Slater Ltd., scrap merchants who had this unique 0-4-0ST. Seen out of use with a steam crane on 25th February 1968, it was built by Markham & Co. of Chesterfield in 1912.
Adrian Booth

Right: The Slag Reduction Company had a slag crushing yard on the east side of the Old Road just north of the site of Woodhouse Mill station.
On Friday 21st March 1969 this Hudswell Clarke 0-4-0ST, works No. 1340, was busy drawing BR wagons loaded with slag through the unloading tippler.
Adrian Booth

Above: The 10.18am Sheffield-Nottingham stopping train leaves Killamarsh Central at 10.50 on Saturday 24th November 1962 with Colwick-based L1 2-6-4T No. 67770 piloting Annesley Stanier Class 5 No. 45116. *Robert Anderson*

Below: Looking north at Treeton on Thursday 2nd August 1979 as Brush Type 2 No. 31316 heads an Up train of engineers' wagons. The sidings on the left form the exchange with the Orgreave coke and chemical plant. They were still there in 2012, but covered by 30ft silver birch trees. *Adrian Booth*

WOODHOUSE MILL: In order to prevent passenger trains being taken into the horse, carriage and cattle dock siding at Woodhouse Mill, vehicles which require to be detached at that station from Up passenger trains must be marshalled in front of the passenger vehicles, and when vehicles are required to be attached by Up passenger trains they must be placed next to the engine. *LMS Sectional Appendix 1937*

Above: A busy scene at the Orgreave coke and chemical works where the British Steel Corporation converted coal into coke for its blast furnaces along with other chemical processes. All were interconnected by a web of railways which was in turn connected to both the Old Road and the GC Sheffield-Retford line. Yorkshire Engine Co. 0-6-0 diesel electric No. 2866, built 1962, shunts the sidings on 1st January 1980. After attaining national infamy during the 1984/85 miners strike as the setting for the so-called "Battle of Orgreave" when miners' pickets and police fought day after day, the works closed in 1991. *Adrian Booth*

Below: Looking north at Treeton Junction on Monday 12th March 1979 as a mixed freight headed by English Electric Type 3 No. 37132 travels south along the Old Road. In the background are loaded MGR wagons awaiting collection from Treeton Colliery, and above them the bridge carrying the industrial line from the colliery to Orgreave works. The passenger station here closed in October 1951 while the semaphores were replaced by multiple aspect signalling in 1982. In 2012, the junction leading left to the District Railway and Tinsley was defunct. *Adrian Booth*

TREETON - ORGREAVES SIDINGS. The signal regulating the running of the NCB engine from the Orgreaves branch is worked by guards and shunters from the ground frame and must always be kept at the Clear position, except when required to be placed to Danger for the protection of trains stopping at the Down sidings for traffic purposes. Trains must not enter the Down sidings from the Down Main at Treeton Junction box. *Eastern Region Sectional Appendix 1969.* A similar instruction appeared in the LMS 1937 Sectional Appendix, except the term "stage" was used instead of "ground frame," the Down Main was referred to as the "Down Passenger," and instead of "NCB engine" it said "Rothervale Colliery Co's engine"

Right: Catcliffe station closed on 11th September 1939 and the goods yard officially on 1st March 1955, by which time it had been used by Wenty's scrap dealers who were cutting up the former North Eastern Railway electric locomotives. After being in store since de-electrification of the Shildon-Newport line, Co. Durham, in the 1930s, these locomotives were considered for use as banking engines on the Manchester, Sheffield & Wath lines. No. 26510 was modified as a prototype and classed EB1 (electric banker 1.) In the event, it was decided to use the EM1s. No. 26505 awaits its fate at Catcliffe in March 1951. Also there were 26502 and 26509. *Alan Ashley*

Below: The east end of Tinsley marshalling yard in 1965 with a WD 2-8-0 that is too filthy to accurately identify, although it looks like 90045 from York. The wagons in the foreground are in the reception sidings. *Tom Greaves*

Above: With modern Tinsley yard's main sorting sidings ranged before it, 8F 2-8-0 No. 48126 looks a little uneasy, perhaps aware that there is no place here for steam locomotives. No steam facilities were provided as it was soon to be eliminated from the Sheffield Division. Any visiting steam loco requiring servicing had to go to Canklow shed, to where steam had been banished. *Tom Greaves*

Below: The diesel servicing depot at Tinsley Yard with all three forms of traction present. From left are: the access line to the diesel maintenance depot with the South West Arrival line passing underneath it, the diesel servicing shed, the loco washer, and the breakdown crane shed. Class 31, 20 and 25 diesel locos are present; the electric loco is 26026 and the steam loco 8F No. 48126, a visitor from Stourton, Leeds. A 45-ton steam breakdown crane, 330102, was stationed here. After locomotive servicing was switched to the maintenance depot in 1984, the overnight cleaning and fuelling of the local DMU fleet of 16 2-car sets was moved here from Darnall. DMU servicing ceased in 1988 when a new depot was built at Sheffield Midland station. A remnant of the South West Arrival line remains in 2013 to provide access from the west end to the Outo Kumpu Tinsley Park stainless steel casting plant. *Tom Greaves*

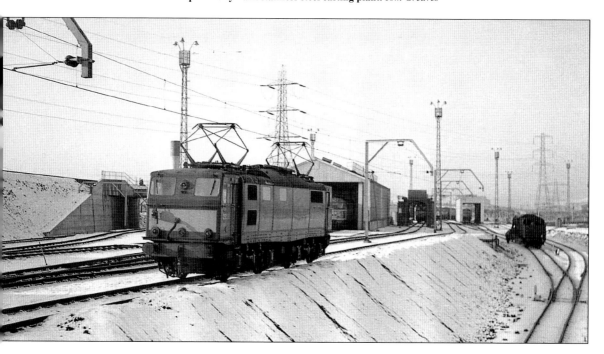

Although on the LNER the District Railway was listed in the 1937 LMS Sectional Appendix. It was signalled by Absolute Block with boxes at(in the Up direction) West Tinsley (1298yds from Brightside Station Jn.,) Tinsley Park Colliery Jn.(1540yds,) Catcliffe (1 mile 704yds,) and Treeton Jn.(990yds.)

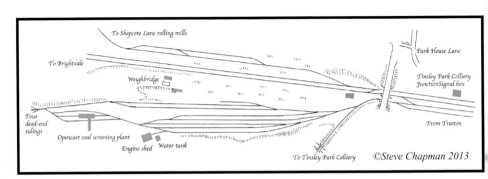

Top: The site of Tinsley marshalling yard as it was in 1955. *Not to scale*

Right: One of the 700hp "Master-Slave" hump shunters stabled in the yard along with standard independent snowplough ADB965211. Medium size vacuum braked plough No. DE330980, mounted on a former steam loco tender, was also based here.
Tom Greaves

Below: Tinsley Yard looking west on Wednesday 3rd April 2002 with the disused main yard control tower dominating a half derelict and overgrown site with what remains of the main sorting sidings in the centre. Since then practically all the sidings have gone, only a few of the express freight and departure roads in the far right distance still being used. The site is now occupied by the Sheffield International Rail Freight Terminal and its 647,000 sq. ft. warehouses which up to the time of writing had seen no rail traffic. Shepcote Lane steel plant in the right distance has been much reduced since this picture. In September 2012 Leicestershire-based Aggregate Industries lodged a planning application for a rail-served aggregates terminal and roadstone manufacturing facility, raising hopes of new rail traffic. *Stephen Chapman*

Above: The east end of Tinsley depot shortly after becoming fully operational, with Brush Type 4 No. D1562 in the foreground. *Tom Greaves*

Cab signalling was one of the numerous advanced features at Tinsley Yard. The Eastern Region Sectional Appendix 1969 stated: "Cab signalling ground equipment has been installed in the Reception Area between the East end of the Reception Sidings and the Hump Summit; the humping units and one standard 350hp diesel shunter are provided with the corresponding cab equipment. These facilities enable the front of a train being propelled towards the hump to proceed safely to a point within a few feet of a ground signal displaying the stop aspect. This permits the time interval between humping of consecutive trains to be reduced to a minimum... the humping units are equipped with a precision speedometer to enable the speed of humping to be accurately regulated. The dial is specially worked to indicate the correct humping speed - 1.36mph(2ft per sec.)......

English Electric Type 3 No. D6816 and a Brush Type 2 at home by the fuelling points on Tinsley maintenance depot shortly after the depot's opening in 1964. *Tom Greaves*

Locomotives allocated to 41A Tinsley May 1965: Brush Type 4: D1550/1/2/3/74/1770-1806; 350hp 0-6-0: D3086/127/9/31/251/2/3/4/88/9/93/574/5/662/98/703/7/27/4028/9/35/6/ 7/8/9/ 40/1/2/3/4/6/7/8/187/8/9/90; Brush Type 2: D5540/1/57/84/682/4/6/7/91/2/840/1/2/ 3/ 4/5/6/ 7/9/850/1/2/5/6/8/61/2; English Electric Type 3: D6742/3/4/5/6/7/8/9/50/1/2/3/4/96/7/ 8/9/ 800-19/959/60/1/2/3/4/5/6/7/8; English Electric Type 1: D8022/3/4/50-69. Total 176

Alex Scott noted the following on Tinsley depot on 3rd January 1965: BR/Sulzer Type 4: D29/40/67; Brush Type 4: D1521/37/8/43/50/1772; 350hp 0-6-0: D3703/4028/9/44; Brush Type 2: D5685/90/1/2/845/51; English Electric Type 3: D6749/98/9; English Electric Type 1: D8023/51/4/7/64/7; Clayton Type 1: D8606/9. Total: 30

Right: The interior of Tinsley depot on Sunday 19th May 1968 with Brush Type 4s (Class 47) Nos. D1521, D1878, D1759 and D1886. *Adrian Booth*

The maintenance shed had six roads at each end with a centrally positioned workshop, administrative and amenities block. Other facilities included overhead cranes while outside were fuelling stages and a washing plant.

The depot was on a higher level than the marshalling yard; access lines to the yard left both the west and east ends of the depot.

Tinsley diesel maintenance depot was completed in January 1964 but restricted access meant it only undertook daily servicing of locomotives until April when it came fully on stream, receiving a large allocation of locomotives and staff transferred from Darnall. It took Darnall's 41A shed code and under the 1970s TOPS system became TI.

Tinsley was originally intended to maintain the Sheffield Division's entire diesel locomotive fleet except those allocated to Wath, and when the transition from steam was complete would have an allocation of about 190 main line locos and 80 shunters. Their numbers were swelled by new locomotives, including the Clayton Type 1s, delivered there until new outbased diesel facilities at Barrow Hill and Shirebrook were ready. In the event, rationalisation saw Tinsley providing locomotives for a much wider area. Although primarily freight, its duties covered everything from humble trip workings to express passenger and it maintained the Sheffield tradition of providing locomotives for summer extras to seaside resorts. In the 1980s it was famously home to the last Class 45 "Peaks" and around that time BR started allowing depots to customise their locos to foster a new spirit of "ownership" by staff. Tinsley took the principle to heart and was famed for the unofficial yet inspiring names it bestowed on its locos. In tribute to the "Peaks" it repainted 45106 in green livery with stainless steel embellishments. Following 45106's withdrawal, Brush 4 No. 47145 became the pet loco, repainted blue, embellished and named *Merddyn Emrys*.

The era of BR business sector management saw Tinsley become dedicated to Railfreight Distribution and was that sector's diesel maintenance centre for all of England and Wales while still maintaining 16 locomotives for the Construction sector. Despite the run-down of the marshalling yard, the depot's future looked secure. But upon privatisation, Railfreight Distribution was sold to English Welsh & Scottish which had already taken over BR's trainload freight operations with such depots as Immingham and Toton. Tinsley was declared surplus and closed in March 1998. By 2013 the site had been totally redeveloped.

The east end of Tinsley depot on Thursday 11th January 1990 with classes 47, 37 and 20 present. Many of the locomotives carry the Railfreight Distribution logo. *Stephen Chapman*

Above: The west end of the depot on the same day with Brush Type 4s, from right, Nos. 47016, 47270 and 47144 present. A single-road extension has been added on the right since the depot was new. *Stephen Chapman*

The main rail access to the complex of works and foundries in the Meadow Hall area was from the District Railway between Brightside and West Tinsley which was on a higher level. The access was awkward and involved steep inclines and various special instructions were issued in the 1969 Sectional Appendix:

E. ALLEN & Co.'s Works: The firm's sidings are situated on the low level and are approached by a single incline leading from the Down sidings....When making movements to the firm's sidings the engine must be attached in rear and if more than 6 wagons are taken down the incline at one time, the Shunter or man in charge must fasten down the brakes of the first 6 wagons. Trains or engines must not exceed...4mph when descending the incline....

FIRTH VICKERS STAINLESS STEELS LTD AND FIRTH DERIHON STAMPINGS LTD. Before any wagons are turned down the incline leading to these works, the brakes of the first 6 must be pinned down.

TINSLEY WORKS BRANCH leading from High Level Down siding shunting spur to Low Level and the Jessop-Saville's works and Hadfield's Ltd. works. The gradient from the shunting spur down the incline siding to the low level is 1 in 40. Not more than 8 loaded or 10 empty wagons must be taken down or brought up the incline at one time. Trains must not exceed 5mph when on the single line branch...... Hadfield's East Hecla works closed in 1984.

The River Don works and its internal railway straddled the A6109 Brightside Lane. Traffic has to wait as 1957-built Hudswell Clarke 0-4-0 diesel, builders No. D996, crosses on Saturday 18th December 1976. Its number plate has been altered from ESC(English Steel Corporation) No. 39 to BSC(British Steel Corporation) No. 39. The River Don works is still in business in 2013 but the railway was abandoned in 1982 when the works merged with Firth Brown's to become Sheffield Forgemasters. *Adrian Booth*

Right: Sheffield was the last city in England to abandon its trams and when it did so in 1960 it left only the seaside town of Blackpool with them.

This view shows 1930s-built 4-wheeled car No. 115 at the Vulcan Road terminus, deep in the Meadow Hall industrial complex in 1960. Hadfield's works can be seen beyond the far tram. *Jack Wild/S. Chapman archive*

Because of the steep hills they had to negotiate, Sheffield trams needed a special braking system which could not be fitted to bogie vehicles so they were quite exceptional in being high capacity cars on 4-wheel trucks.

At the end of the District Railway branch from Brightside, Attercliffe was listed in the 1956 Handbook of Stations as having a 35-ton crane capacity and equipped to handle general goods.

Private sidings served: Cox & Danks Ltd.; Industrial Steels Ltd.; Esso fuel depot; Fina Fuel Products Ltd.; Hadfields Ltd.; Sanderson Bros. & Newboulds; Sheffield Chemical Co.; and Woodhouse & Rixon's Chantry Steel & Crank works.

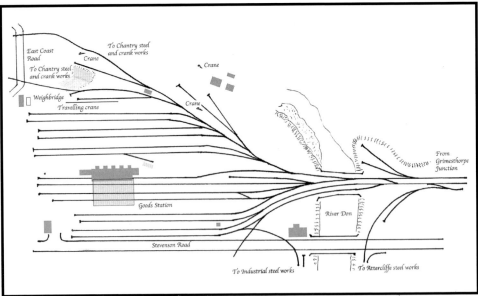

Left: The layout at Attercliffe goods yard as it was in 1935. *Not to scale.*

It outlived the 1960s goods yard closures but by 1968 the goods station had been demolished. The yard was eventually taken over by Cooper's Metals, now part of European Metal Recycling, and in 2013 remains one of the very few active private sidings in the Sheffield area.

SANDERSON BROS AND NEWBOULD'S SIDINGS. The gradient falls from Attercliffe Yard to Stevenson Road gates at 1 in 30, crosses the road on the level and then falls from the road at 1 in 30 towards Sanderson's Works. Not more than 10 wagons for Sanderson's Works must be propelled at one time, speed not to exceed 4mph.......Before any wagon or engine is allowed to enter upon Stevenson Road, either to or from Sanderson's sidings, the Shunter in charge must arrange for a man with a red flag by day, or red light by night, to be stationed in the road to stop traffic and pedestrians. The handsignalman in Stevenson Road must not be withdrawn until the wagons are safely clear of Industrial Steel Co.'s gates and clear in Cattle Dock Siding, when he must close and lock the gate on the Goods Yard side of Stevenson Road....*Eastern Region Sectional Appendix 1969*

The Appendix also instructed that wagons for the Industrial Steel Co's sidings must be propelled from the Cattle Dock Siding across Stevenson Road and placed in the siding clear of the vehicular crossing, the wagon brakes being fastened down and left secure. The same instruction applied regarding the appointing and withdrawal of a hand signalman at the road crossing.